FOREWORD

On 28 January 2016, ESCWA and the Centre for Syrian Studies at the University of St Andrews signed a letter of understanding on joint scholarly activity, which aims at promoting a deeper understanding of the Syrian crisis and how to build a politically inclusive Syria that gives all of citizens the opportunity to pursue a life free from poverty and fear.

Since the crisis began in March 2011, ESCWA and the Centre for Syrian Studies have sought to strike out along a path of scholarly research rather than politicised rhetoric, focused on what can be done rather than on who is to blame. By so doing, they have put themselves in a position that qualifies them to produce a joint report that provides a diagnosis and a prescription to all those concerned about Syria's future, irrespective of their political background or affiliation.The report benefits from extensive research undertaken in the framework of The National Agenda for the Future of Syria (NAFS), which brings together hundreds of Syrian and international experts in a mammoth effort to chart the steps to be taken after the conflict ends. The overarching concepts include not only reconstruction and development, but an emphasis on human rights, social justice and an inclusive society in which all can resolve their grievances peacefully, thereby paving the way for rapid human development.

The report provides thorough documentation of the impact of five years of violence and war on Syria's economy, and pays special attention to the plight of refugees and the extent to which Western sanctions have succeeded, or failed, in achieving their proclaimed objectives. Although the report is essentially focused on the socioeconomic consequences of the conflict, it goes further and provides several guiding principles and a preliminary action plan focused on the period immediately following an agreement on a political resolution to the crisis. It also offers valuable prescriptions by which the international community could, in the immediate term, mitigate the human damage caused by the crisis.

If this report contributes, however minimally, to an understanding of the costs of the Syrian crisis and thereby prevents its reoccurrence, in Syria or elsewhere, it will have far exceeded expectations.

Abdallah Al-Dardari   **Raymond Hinnebusch**

ACKNOWLEDGMENTS

This report constitutes a joint effort by ESCWA and the University of St Andrews. Abdallah Al-Dardari (Deputy Executive Secretary of ESCWA) and Raymond Hinnebusch (Director of the Centre for Syrian Studies at the University of St Andrews) oversaw its preparation.

The lead authors of the report are: Khalid Abu-Ismail, Omar Imady, Aljaz Kuncic, Osama Nojoum and Justine Walker; with important contributions from Mohamed Asadi, Ahmad Shikh Ebid and Bayan El-Mihthawi.

Special thanks go to Joma'a Hijazi for his rich data and analysis of human development and macroeconomics in Syria.

The lead authors are grateful for the contributions, background papers and research carried out by the National Agenda for the Future of Syria (NAFS). We are also grateful to the NAFS team for its tremendous support: Bassel Kaghadou for managerial support and substantive contributions, Riad Sabbagh for guidance on communications and outreach, and Rania Nasser for coordination.

Thanks also go to Yarob Badr, Niranjan Sarangi and Mahdi Al-Dajani for their constructive review of the first draft of this report, to Damien Simonis for editing and advice, to Fouad Ghorra for graphs and referencing support and to Maral Tashjian for administrative assistance.

The opinions expressed are those of the authors and do not necessarily reflect the views of the Secretariat of the United Nations or the University of St Andrews.

Lead authors

**Khalid Abu-Ismail,
Omar Imady,
Aljaz Kuncic,
Osama Nojoum,
Justine Walker**

CONTENTS

5

LIST OF FIGURES

INTRODUCTION

Five years of conflict have changed the face of the Syrian Arab Republic. The numbers are eloquent. An estimated 2.3 million people, 11.5 per cent of the country's population, have been killed or wounded,[1] thousands more are under arrest or unaccounted for, 6.5 million are internally displaced and 6.1 million have sought refuge in neighbouring countries. Gross domestic product (GDP), which in 2010 stood at $60.2 billion, is now at $27.2 billion (2010 prices), representing a contraction of 55 per cent. Total losses incurred in five years of conflict are estimated at $259.6 billion. Destruction of housing and infrastructure is estimated at around $90 billion. The total area under cultivation has fallen by 40 per cent and one third of the population inside Syria does not have food security. No economic sector has been spared and the impact of sanctions has been considerable. More than 80 per cent of the population is living below the poverty line (28 per cent in 2010). Millions are deprived of the essential necessities of life: 13.5 million are in need of human assistance and 12.1 million lack adequate access to water, sanitation and waste disposal. Around half of Syria's hospitals have sustained serious damage. According to one estimate, life expectancy dropped from 70 in 2010 to 55.4 in 2014.[2] Thousands of schools have ceased to operate and an estimated 2.7 million school-age children are out of school inside and outside Syria, with the rate of primary enrolment down from nearly 100 per cent in 2010 to 60 per cent today.

The degree of fragmentation is such that analysts speak of "economies" and administrative structures operating outside of Government authority. Other factors are far more difficult to quantify: psychological trauma, the disempowerment of women and, perhaps most importantly, the deep divides in Syrian society. It is important to understand how all this came to pass, not only to avoid its reoccurrence in Syria, but also to prevent it from happening in other countries.

Various political, economic and legal/administrative reasons, as well as external factors, have been posited in order to explain how and why the crisis unfolded in Syria. Political explanations focus on how the Damascus Spring was suppressed in 2001, the slow pace of democratic reform, the Government's reaction to initial protests in the months following March 2011, and the use of overwhelming force by the army after July 2011. Economic reasons include rural poverty, the devastating drought prior to 2011, now regarded as the worst in centuries,[3] corruption and the perception of severe inequality in terms of income distribution. Legal/administrative explanations focus on the yawning gap between the avowed aims of policymakers before the crisis, and what they actually achieved, in particular with respect to the failure to put reforms that had been introduced into practice. Among the most telling external factors was the role of regional powers in inflaming and perpetuating the fighting. However, none of those factors, taken separately or in combination, is enough to explain the type and intensity of the conflict.

Syria in 2011 was certainly no fully fledged democracy, but 1,461 civil associations, more than 500 of them based in Damascus, were active on the eve of the crisis.[4] Outright political dissent was not tolerated, but criticism of Government performance in official and unofficial media was widespread.

In the run-up to March 2011, GDP had grown significantly and officials were openly discussing poverty, especially in rural areas, and how to measure and tackle the problem. Through official, semi-official and voluntary channels, millions of dollars had been dispensed as income-generating loans, often accompanied by technical expertise. A commission for combating unemployment had also been set up.

The need to improve governance significantly had been recognized. Administrative structures had been established and international expertise sought in order to implement the necessary changes. Numerous presidential decrees signed in the period leading up to 2011 addressed issues that had long been ignored. Laws were passed enabling the establishment of private banks and universities and, for the first time since 1963, the stock exchange reopened. Far from being aligned with one regional power, the Islamic Republic of Iran, Syria had seemingly resolved long-standing problems with Turkey, and trade and cultural ties between the two countries were flourishing.

In short, much about the position of Syria in March 2011 was positive, and it could be argued that the future held the promise of further development and improvement.

The Arab uprisings that started in late 2010 had the effect of a sudden, powerful earthquake. Many structures were shattered or underwent significant damage. In Syria, it was as though the very earth had fractured along deep societal fault lines. Those fault lines largely shaped the way in which events developed and were perceived by all major groups after March 2011. Understanding how those fault lines emerged requires a brief historical overview of Syria's recent political past.

After the collapse of the Ottoman empire in 1918 and the arrival of King Faisal and the Arab army in Damascus, the first general Syrian conference was held in May 1919. It constituted the foundation of what would come to be known as modern Syria. In March 1920, that same body declared Syria's independence and 85 delegates from four regions adopted a Constitution four months later. In it, Syria was proclaimed an administratively decentralized State with a civil constitutional monarchy in which executive, legislative and judicial powers were separated. The equal treatment of all citizens, irrespective of their religion, sect or ethnicity, was enshrined in its articles and women were guaranteed the right to vote and run for office.[5] In the Constitution, Islam was specified as the religion of the Hashemite Monarch but there was no reference to religion as a basis for legislation. The civil nature of the State was thus ensured.

That progressive experiment in State-building was brought to a swift end in July 1920 by the arrival of French forces. Moreover, the authorities of the French Mandate, which lasted until April 1946, deliberately sought to accentuate differences between various ethnic and religious groups in Syria, often playing one group against the other. The allocation of a distinct, often autonomous, status to groups that had been marginalised during the Ottoman era did not contribute to the creation of a cohesive State, nor did it foster harmony among Syria's citizens.

Democratically elected post-independence Governments failed to appreciate that, against that background, they had to reach out with a comprehensive economic and social programme to Syria's rural areas, where the majority of its marginalised groups lived in poverty, without education or infrastructure and exposed to disease.[6] By 1950, it had become apparent that the attention of those Governments was caught up in urban elitist interests. They simply could not see the importance of offering all Syrians equal opportunities for political and economic empowerment. The unintended message was that democratic elections were bound to produce Governments indifferent to the plight of marginalised groups. Rural youth, especially in coastal areas, turned increasingly to the one reliable source of regular pay: the armed forces. By 1963, they were strong enough to bring the Arab Socialist Ba'ath Party into power and, by 1970, had fully consolidated their authority. The Ba'ath party succeeded where other parties failed not only because it had attracted many influential army officers, but also because it was particularly attractive to members of marginalised groups.

Indeed, under the Ba'ath, rural areas received far more attention than they had in the past. In addition to land reforms, the Government invested heavily in bringing electricity, roads and schools to areas that had been neglected previously. At the same time, however, all forms of genuine political dissent were crushed, often ruthlessly, and important segments of the population felt that their values were being deliberately undermined. That sense of dissatisfaction eventually culminated in the Muslim Brotherhood insurgency and the tragic events of 1982 in Hama, where thousands of civilians were killed as the Government retook control of the city. Society was by now deeply divided, and no one seemed to have the vision required to escape the trap of interacting on the basis of sect, class or ethnicity. What primarily mattered to the Government was authority and control, and as long as those societal divides did not constitute a serious challenge, they were ignored. Indeed, the more the legacy of the past was ignored, the more it became part of the present.

When Bashar al-Assad was sworn in as Syria's president on 24 July 2000, the violence of the 1980s seemed a distant memory. However, a serious wound had yet to be healed. More than political, administrative and economic reform, Syria was in dire need of a courageous attempt to acknowledge the sectarian and ethnic injustices and violence of its recent past. At the least, steps should have been taken to address the grievances of those with missing family members, or whose property had been confiscated or damaged. Policymakers failed to see that a country in which segments of the population believe they have been gravely mistreated will prove vulnerable when dramatic events occur.

In March 2011, Syria was confronted by the one challenge it was not prepared to face. On every other level, although with shortcomings and in need of reforms, Syria could not seriously have been described as vulnerable. Yet, the house that was Syria was built on soft sand. It was unable to withstand the earthquake of 2011.

In the pages that follow, indicators based on extensive field research tell the story of the aftermath of five years of violence and war. Special focus is given to the impact of sanctions, and the plight of refugees and its repercussions for regional countries and Europe. The numbers point to significant loss and destruction, but one might have expected a good deal worse. That Syria still has elements of a working economy and a currency that has not entirely collapsed shows how solid certain aspects of the Syrian State were in early 2011. Sadly, however, it was unprepared where it mattered most.

The report is structured as follows: Section 1 focuses on economic and social indicators, contrasting where Syria was in regard to those indicators on the eve of this crisis and where it is after five years of violence and destruction. Section 2 examines the European Union's socioeconomic cooperation with Syria, the flow of refugees and migrants to Syria's neighbours and Europe, and the impact of sanctions on the Syrian people. Finally, Section 3 identifies guiding principles and key critical steps for post-conflict Syria. Policy recommendations are included throughout.

11

SYRIA TODAY
WHERE ARE WE NOW?

1.1 BEFORE THE WAR

By 2011, Syria had arguably made great strides, at least quantitatively, in terms of social development. With the same level of income per capita as in Egypt, Syria had nearly half the rate of poverty. It had made greater progress on the Millennium Development Goals (MDGs) than most other Arab countries, with notable success in critical areas such as food security, infant mortality and access to education, particularly for girls.[7]

The Syrian economy was relatively healthy, with per capita income growth above the global average. It had shown resilience over the previous decade in the face of global (food and financial crises), regional (Iraqi refugees and the war in Lebanon) and domestic (drought) problems. However, although the economy was able to compensate for declining agricultural production with increases in the output of other sectors, the drought had enormous social and demographic repercussions, causing internal migration and impoverishing hundreds of thousands of rural dwellers.[8]

Growth driven by rising consumption and exports of oil and services led to an increase in official foreign currency reserves. They reached a record high in 2010. Foreign debt also declined significantly. The Syrian pound was stable and inflation was moderate.

Liberalization measures also spurred foreign trade with reduced tariff and non-tariff barriers.[9] The combined value of exports and imports of goods averaged 60 per cent of GDP between 2006 and 2010, an indicator of a relatively open economy. The trade deficit, as in many other Arab countries, averaged 8 per cent over the same period.[10]

In line with new market-led policies, subsidies (such as on fuel, food and agricultural supplies) were lowered, which also made sense given that Syria's oil reserves are limited. Average yearly non-oil tax revenue rose from 38 per cent of total public revenue between 2000 and 2005 to 47 per cent between 2006 and 2010. The average share of non-oil and non-tax revenue increased from 17 per cent to 27 per cent over the same period. However, widespread tax evasion meant that the contribution of direct taxes (especially tax on income and profit) to total revenues dropped from 31 per cent in 2000 to 14 per cent in 2010.[11] Trade, tourism and banking grew rapidly before the crisis. The exchange rate was stable at about 50 Syrian pounds to one US dollar. Bank deposits increased by 10 per cent annually from 2005 to 2010 and inflation was moderate (annual average of 4.5 per cent) in the same period.[12]

In short, the macroeconomic environment was stable in the decade prior to the conflict. Low national debt made it possible to embark on a major programme to modernize institutions and upgrade infrastructure. There were no doubt major economic policy challenges. Paramount among them was chronic youth unemployment and the dearth of decent jobs. The drought had highlighted the inability of the State to respond effectively to crises. Fiscal policy needed fundamental revision, particularly in terms of transparency and accountability. Monetary policy needed to be aligned with development policy. Most of all, there was a perceived growing disparity in income and wealth between rural and urban areas and within the latter between the middle class (who formed the majority of the population in 2010) and the new rich class of politically well connected entrepreneurs.[13]

1.2   THE ECONOMY

1.2.1   NEGATIVE GDP GROWTH AND SIGNIFICANT DAMAGE TO CAPITAL STOCK

Cumulative losses during between 2011 and 2015 are estimated at $259.6 billion, $169.7 billion in GDP[14] and $89.9 billion in capital stock.[15] GDP losses accelerated in 2012 and 2013 as economic activity plummeted and fighting intensified and spread across the country. Economic sanctions began to bite in mid-2012, affecting all economic sectors, especially those dependent on primary production materials, food products and fuel. The collapse in oil (from 386,000 to 28,000 barrels a day) and natural gas (from 8.9 billion cubic meters to 5.9 billion cubic meters) production between 2010 and 2013 exacerbated GDP losses.[16]

Figure 1: Real GDP losses (billions of US dollars in 2010 prices)

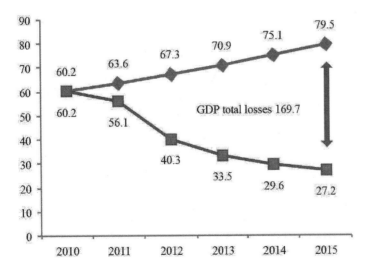

Source: Data from ESCWA National Agenda for the Future of Syria (NAFS) and the eleventh five-year plan (Syrian State Planning Commission, 2011).

Real GDP contracted by 55 per cent between 2010 and 2015, when it had been expected to grow by 32 per cent. The heftiest decline took place in 2012 and 2013, with falls of 28.2 per cent and 16.7 per cent respectively (figure 2).

Some economic activities came back to life as the security situation improved in parts of Damascus, Lattakia and Tartus, and as a result of aid from countries such as the Islamic Republic of Iran and the Russian Federation. Even so, GDP is expected to have fallen by a further 8 per cent in 2015. According to the Syrian Center for Policy Research (SCPR), GDP losses in 2011-2015 were concentrated in domestic trade, Government services and the oil and gas sectors, in that order.

The destruction of physical capital has been devastating. The construction sector has sustained the heaviest damage, reaching $27.2 billion, or around one third of total losses (figure 3). Manufacturing has been the second hardest hit, with capital losses estimated at $15.9 billion, mostly in facilities in Aleppo, Damascus and Homs. Destruction of oil and gas fields is estimated at $8.4 billion, and that of electricity, water and sewage installations at $8.2 billion.

Figure 2: GDP losses and projected growth in the absence of conflict

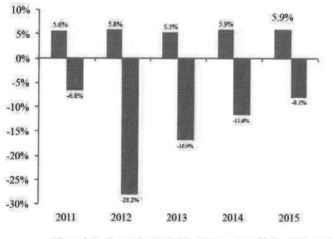

Source: Data from NAFS.

Figure 3: Capital stock losses, 2011-2015 (percentages, billions of US dollars)

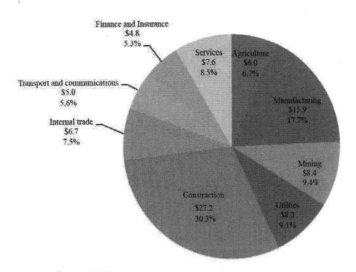

Source: Data from NAFS.

The informal economy tends to flourish in times of unrest and war. In Syria, it is thought that the informal economy before the crisis already represented around 40 per cent of GDP. It is likely to have grown considerably in areas outside Government control, especially in the north, northeast and south, and in some areas along the border with Lebanon.

Informal activities have also become more widespread in some Government-held areas not fully controlled by the authorities, and have been encouraged by interruptions in the supply of goods and services.

The income generated by such activities and crime (kidnapping, theft, vandalism and illegal trade) is difficult to estimate and thus not included in the above GDP estimates.

Some estimates are, however, available. According to the self-styled Islamic State, Deir el-Zor province, almost entirely under its control, had an annual budget of $2 billion, with a surplus of $250 million. Daily revenue in February 2015 was $8.4 million, of which $2 million each came from oil and taxes, $342,000 from gas, and $3.7 million from confiscations (figure 4).

Figure 4: Daily revenues claimed by Islamic State in Deir el-Zor, February 2015 (in millions of US dollars)

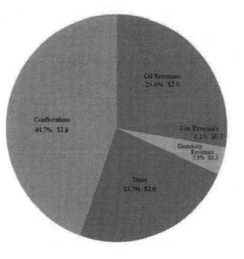

Source: Mohamed, A. (2015). "The ISIS Economy: Lasting and expanding", December. Beirut: Lebanese American University.

1.2.2 SHRINKING AGRICULTURAL PRODUCTION AND WIDESPREAD FOOD INSECURITY

Before the conflict, Syria did not rely on food imports. However, farming GDP fell by nearly 60 per cent in real terms between 2010 and 2015. Many factors contributed to the decline, including: the lack of access to farmland due to military operations; the lack or expense of energy sources needed for irrigation; the impact of sanctions on production costs; the destruction of farms; and the rising cost of transport. The total area under cultivation dropped from 6 million to 3.6 million hectares and land productivity plummeted.[17]

As a result, the price of food in Syria has risen sharply, especially since 2014. For example, the wholesale price of a metric ton of wheat in Damascus in 2015 was $444, nearly triple the global average of $157.70. Food prices rose on average by 62.1 per cent between November 2014 and November 2015, although regional variations were tremendous (from 46.5 per cent in Damascus to 978 per cent in Deir el-Zor). The price of wheat flour and rice rose by 43 per cent and 89 per cent respectively between 2014 and 2015. The rise since March 2011 for those products has been even more dramatic: 388 per cent and 723 per cent respectively (figures 5a and b).

Figure 5: Price inflation for basic goods

A: November 2014-November 2015

B: March 2011-November 2015

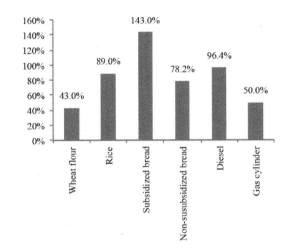

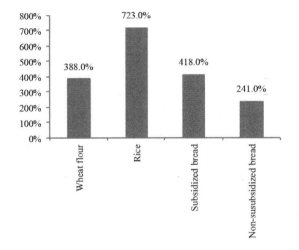

Source: World Food Programme (2015b), Market Price Watch Bulletin. November. Issue 2.

In spite of efforts by international organizations to provide food aid to needy displaced and resident populations, the situation has deteriorated significantly, especially since 2014. The fact that the World Food Programme (WFP) and other partners provided food-related assistance to some six million Syrians in 2015 speaks volumes (figure 6).[18] In the course of the conflict, 16 per cent of Syrians have slept without a meal more than 10 times a month and 45 per cent from 3 to 10 times a month.

Figure 6: Food security during the conflict

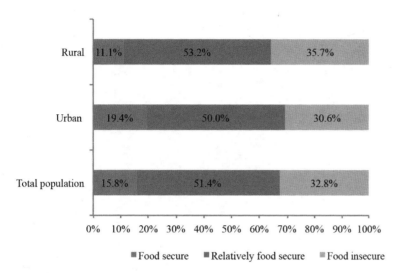

Source: World Food Programme (2015a), Food Security Assessment Report, Syria. October.

1.2.3   FISCAL IMPACT OF THE CONFLICT

Conflict has led to escalating budget deficits, especially since 2012, when State revenues began to plummet (figure 7a). Current expenditure, the largest component of public spending, fell by 52 per cent in real terms, and capital spending collapsed by 95 per cent (figure 7b). Expenditure on subsidies and transfers fell in real terms from 285 billion pounds in 2012 to 160 billion pounds in 2015 (figure 8a), while before 2012 the availability of data is limited to transfers and expenditures for price stabilization fund. Salaries and wages made up the largest share of current expenditure, followed by transfers and subsides.[19]

Oil revenues decreased by 95 per cent in constant prices as oil and gas production collapsed (figure 8b) in the wake of the loss by the Government of control over a large number of oil fields and the destruction of transport routes.[20]

Non-oil revenues also fell by 95 per cent in constant prices, due to the decline in economic activity and withholding of tax and fee payments.[21]

Figure 7: Budget deficits (A): Current and capital expenditure (B): in 2010 prices

(A) **(B)**

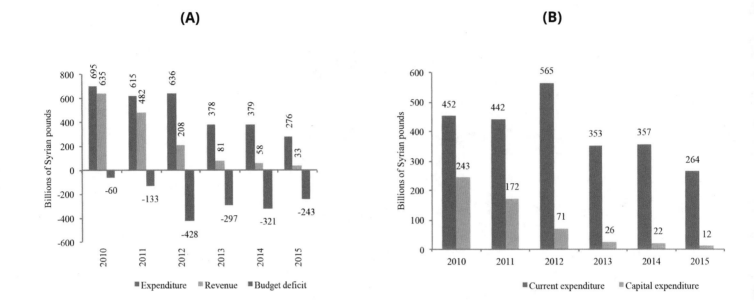

Source: Date from NAFS.

Note: The constant prices deflated using the black market exchange rate.

Figure 8: Current expenditure breakdown (A): Oil and non-oil revenues (B): In 2010 prices

(A) **(B)**

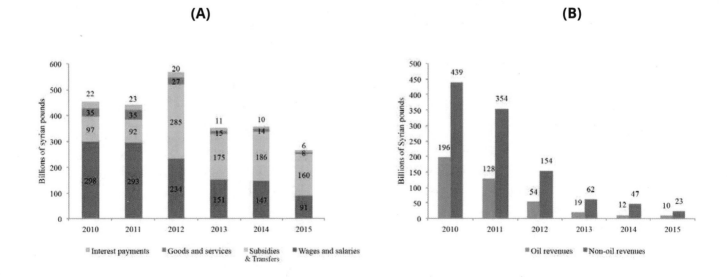

Source: Data from NAFS.

Revenue has collapsed over the five years of conflict but there has been no commensurate decline in expenditure. In fact, even in real terms, expenditure on subsidies (mainly for food and fuel) has risen since 2010 in an attempt to cushion the rising cost of the war. As a result, public debt has blown out in nominal terms (from 651 million pounds in 2010 to more than 5.5 trillion pounds in 2015). However, when converted to constant 2010 prices, the increase is less conspicuous and if we use the exchange rate as a deflator, it may not have changed much since 2010 (figure 9).

Figure 9: Public debt in nominal prices, 2010-2015 (trillions of Syrian pounds)

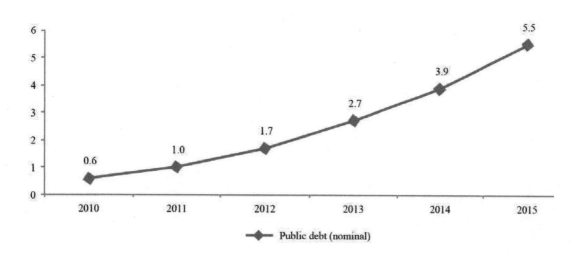

Source: Data from NAFS.

1.2.4 TRADE CONTRACTION, DOMESTIC RECESSION AND SANCTIONS

The economic slowdown and sanctions have had a direct impact on foreign trade. Exports and imports fell by 89 per cent and 60 per cent respectively between 2011 and 2014 (in current US dollar terms). Those falls were not reflected in a similar decrease in the trade deficit (figure 10a),[22] meaning that official exchange reserves have been exhausted by financing imports.

China led suppliers of goods to Syria between 2011 and 2014, followed by Turkey and the Russian Federation (figure 10b). Germany, Italy and Iraq were the top three importing countries for Syrian goods (figure 10c) over the same period. However, the order of Syria's main trade partners changed between 2010 and 2014. In 2010, Iraq, Italy and Germany accounted for 29 per cent, 18 per cent and 18 per cent of all Syrian exports, and Turkey, China and Italy accounted for 10 per cent, 9 per cent and 8 per cent of all imports to Syria respectively.

In spite of border closures and question marks over relations between Syria and Turkey, the latter advanced its position and accounted for 26 per cent ($1.8 billion) of the former's imports in 2014. China's role as an exporter to Syria declined, settling at 14 per cent, while Italy's share of imports into Syria had dropped to just 3 per cent of the total by 2014, largely due to sanctions.[23] Syrian exports in the years 2011-2014 were dominated by oil products, raw materials such as salt, plaster and stone, and farm products such as fruit, vegetables and cotton (figure 10d). Imports were more diversified (figure 10e).

Conflict and sanctions have led Syria to cut imports, even of essential items such as food.

Figure 10: Impact of the conflict on trade, 2011-2014

A: Exports, imports and trade deficit

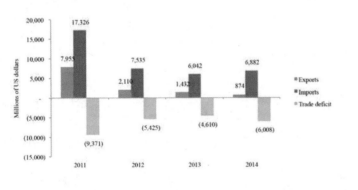

B: Top suppliers of goods to Syria, cumulative 2011-2014

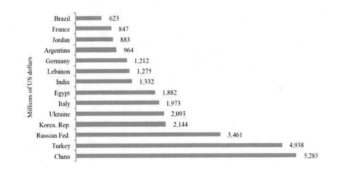

C: Top destination countries of Syrian exports, cumulative 2011-2014

D: Top imported commodities to Syria in 2011

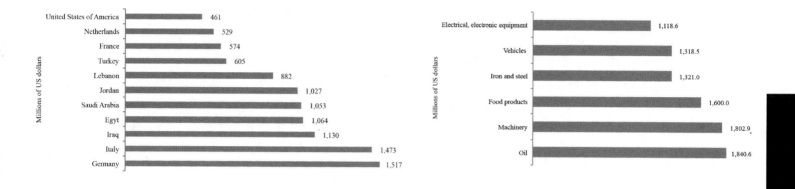

E: Top imported commodities to Syria in 2014

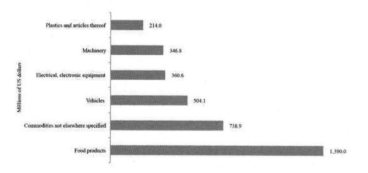

Source: International Trade Centre (ITC) calculations based on UN Comtrade statistics.

Note: All figures in current US dollars.

1.2.5 INFLATION, DEVALUATION AND SUPPLY SHORTAGES

Fiscal and trade deficits have eaten into official foreign currency reserves. At the outbreak of hostilities, the Central Bank of Syria had an estimated $22-24 billion in official reserves. After three years of fighting, it had used up more than $14 billion. The nominal exchange rate of the Syrian pound fell as the war intensified, sanctions were applied and the demand for foreign currency by potential refugees rose. Currency operations also expanded in the parallel market inside Syria and in neighbouring countries. The economic policy response was to curtail demand for foreign currency by rationalizing imports and to manage supply of foreign currency through Central Bank interventions, mainly the sale of foreign currency in the market through a bidding process. The conflict also brought steep rises in domestic prices. Inflation peaked in 2013 at almost 90 per cent and was still at 43 per cent in 2015 (figure 11b).

Figure 11: Consumer prices and exchange rates

A: Consumer price index (CPI) and exchange rates (Syrian pound to US dollar)   **B: Inflation**

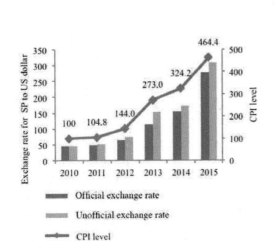

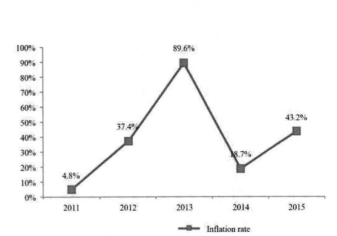

Source: Data from NAFS.

Notes: Base year 2010=100; SP = Syrian pound.

As the conflict intensified, particularly after the international coalition started air strikes on Syrian targets, downward pressure on the value of the Syrian pound grew, in spite of the

Central Bank's efforts to prop it up. Between March 2011 and the end of 2015, the official nominal exchange rate weakened (increased) by 647 per cent, and the unofficial rate by 714 per cent (figure 12a). The real value of the pound (based on the World Bank indicator for the group of basic goods except energy on the base year of 2010), however, has not fallen below 60 pounds to the US dollar (figure 12b). There has also been a sizeable influx of foreign exchange, mostly unofficial, into the country during the five years of conflict.

Figure 12: Exchange rate during the conflict

A: Syrian pound to US dollar (official and parallel exchange rates)

B: Real exchange rate of Syrian pound to US dollar

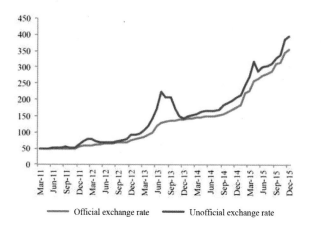

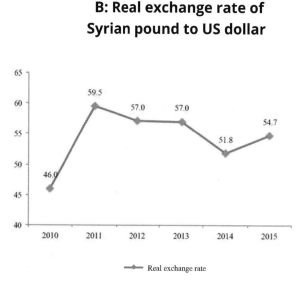

Source: Data from NAFS.

1.3 IMPACT ON THE SYRIAN PEOPLE

Five years of brutal conflict in Syria have been sufficient to wreck development gains accumulated over the previous 25 years, worsening the living conditions of the vast majority of the population and sending many Syrian families into poverty. Education institutions, healthcare facilities and utilities have all suffered damage. Public services have deteriorated in quantity and quality, even in relatively secure areas overloaded due to the growing numbers of internally displaced persons (IDPs). Social structures have been shattered as almost half the population has been forced to flee abroad or within the country.

1.3.1   THE POPULATION

Of an estimated total population of 22 million, 6.5 million were internally displaced in 2015, most of them in the governorates of Aleppo and rural Damascus (figure 13). According to the Assessment Capacities Project (ACAPS), approximately 1.7 million IDPs were living in camps in 2015, and 360,000 were in areas under siege.

Figure 13: Internally displaced population (IDPs) by governorate, 2015

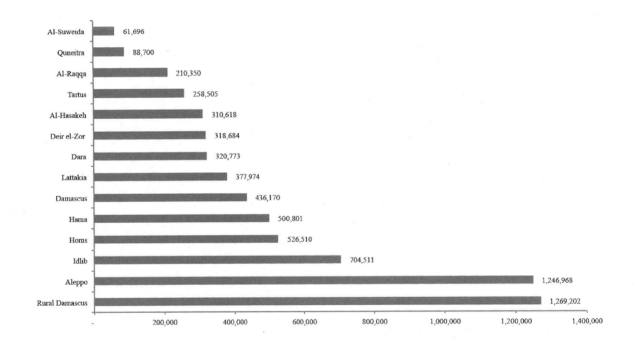

Source: United Nations Office for the Coordination of Humanitarian Affairs (OCHA), 2015. Humanitarian response plan: January-December 2016. Syrian Arab Republic.

The number of Syrians in neighbouring countries (Egypt, Iraq, Jordan, Lebanon and Turkey) was thought to exceed 6 million by the end of November 2015 (figure 14a). Almost 5 million refugees were officially registered (figure 14b).

Figure 14: Syrian refugees

A: Syrian refugees in neighbouring countries

Egypt, 260,000
4.2%

Lebanon, 1,500,000
24.4%

Jordan, 1,400,000
22.7%

Iraq, 250,000
4.1%

Turkey, 2,750,000
44.6%

B: Officially registered Syrian refugees in neighbouring countries

Egypt
118,512
2.5%

Iraq 245,543
5.1%

Jordan
639,704
13.4%

Lebanon
1,067,785
22.3%

Turkey
2,715,789
56.7%

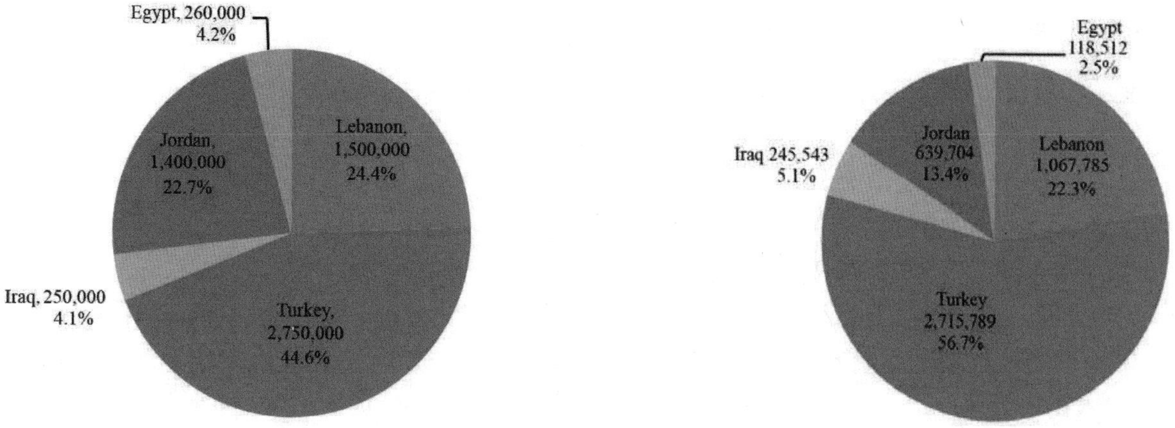

Source: Office of the United Nations High Commissioner for Refugees (UNCHR), 2016a. 3RP Regional Refugee & Resilience Plan 2016-2017: In response to the Syria crisis.

1.3.2 SOURCES OF INCOME AND EMPLOYMENT

In 2015, salaries (in the formal and informal sectors) and pensions were the main source of income for 58 per cent of Syrians, down from 68 per cent in 2013. The drop can be attributed to the closure of many labour-intensive establishments because of the conflict. The proportion of households depending on income generated by the self-employed increased from 26 per cent to 33.7 per cent during the same period.

Growing dependence on more uncertain sources of income, such as through self-employment, remittances and humanitarian aid, combined with the deteriorating purchasing power of local currency, has forced many households to develop different coping strategies in order to cover their basic needs. One out of three households had to borrow from relatives or friends to cover their food, housing, health and education needs in the first half of 2015, and 17 per cent of households were forced to sell one or more of their durable goods to obtain food and other essentials. More seriously, 10 per cent of households had to sell a productive asset (sewing machine, irrigation equipment, livestock, car or a bike) used to generate income in order to meet their basic needs, according to the Syrian Central Bureau of Statistics.

Much of the deterioration in income sources can be ascribed to structural changes in the labour market as most young people over the age of 18 years have been driven into military service. Moreover, the closure of many workplaces has led to massive job losses. Indeed, the economy lost 2.1 million actual and potential jobs between 2010 and 2015. Unemployment in 2015 was 55 per cent, up from 54.2 per cent in 2013. Youth unemployment soared from 69 per cent in 2013 to 78 per cent in 2015. Households in Aleppo and Dara governorates have lost more jobs relative to other governorates.[24]

1.3.3   POVERTY AND PEOPLE IN NEED OF HUMANITARIAN AID

Falling income, widespread unemployment and diminished purchasing power mean rising poverty. Measuring poverty in Syria today is complex. It has been estimated that 83.4 per cent of Syrians now live below the upper (moderate) poverty line applied by the Government of Syria, up from 28 per cent in 2010 (figure 15a).[25] A large share of the employed population may thus be considered as the working poor. This is largely because the cost of the standard food basket has risen more than threefold in nominal terms since 2010, and modest rises in nominal salaries have absorbed only 15-20 per cent of the price increases.[26] Extreme poverty is also projected to have increased from approximately 14 per cent in 2010 to more than 50 per cent of the population in 2015 (authors' estimates).

The poverty gap has deepened.[27] In 2010, poverty in Syria was considered "shallow". In other words, most of the poor had expenditure that was close to the poverty line and thus relatively little effort was needed to lift them above that line. That is no longer the case. The poverty gap reached a new record in 2015 of 16.3 per cent, up from 11.9 per cent in 2013. The gap was worst in rural areas at 17.9 per cent, up from 13.6 per cent in 2013 (figure 15b).

Figure 15: Poverty

A: Population below the upper poverty line

B: Poverty gap ratio, 2010-2015

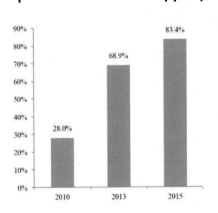

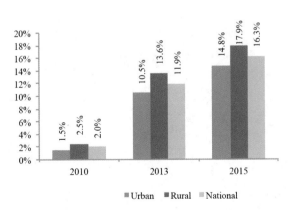

Source: ESCWA estimates based on data from the Syrian Central Bureau of Statistics.

By the end of 2015, an estimated 13.5 million people (3.8 million men, 3.7 million women and 6 million children) in Syria were in need of one form or another of humanitarian aid (up from 1 million in June 2012), of whom 12.1 million needed access to water, sanitation and waste disposal (figure 16a). More than 4 million were concentrated in the governorates of Damascus and Aleppo (figure 16b).

Figure 16: Population in need of humanitarian aid, 2015

A: By type of intervention

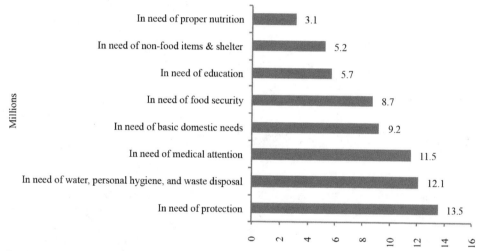

B: By governorate

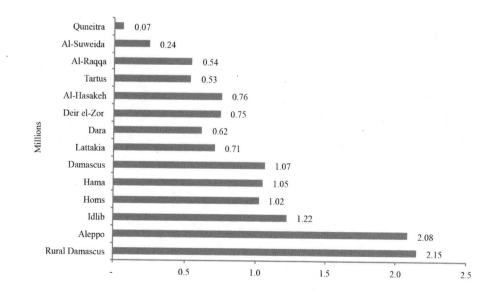

Sources: ACAPS, 2015. Syria crisis: scenarios, possible developments in Syria over the next 12 months. November; and OCHA, 2015. Humanitarian response plan: January-December 2016. Syrian Arab Republic.

1.3.4   EDUCATION

The devastating impact of conflict on education in Syria, wiping out decades of development, threatens to leave an entire generation of children without education. The portion of the population with access to education fell from 95 per cent prior to the crisis to less than 75 per cent in 2015, a result of the loss of infrastructure and a shortage of teachers. More than 27 per cent of schools reported staff shortages in 2015, as opposed to 0.3 per cent in 2010.[28]

According to the Syrian Ministry of Education, 5,800 schools (26 per cent of the national total) were out of action in 2015, due to destruction and inaccessibility (5,200) or because they were being used as shelters for IDPs (600). Government expenditure on education has fallen from an average 5 per cent of GDP in 2000-2010 to 3 per cent since 2011. It should be borne in mind that GDP shrank considerably between the two periods.[29]

All the above has led to disastrous rates of school attendance. By 2015, many children had been out of school for several years. Around 2 million school-age children are not attending school in Syria and another 446,000 are at risk of dropping out.

At the same time, 713,000 refugee children (53 per cent of all school-aged refugee children) are not enrolled in school in neighbouring countries. One fifth of those who do attend school are in informal schools.[30] The national ratio of enrolment in primary education fell from 98 per cent in 2010 to 70 per cent in 2013 and further to 61.5 per cent in 2015 (figure 17a).

However, the ratio of female to male enrolment in all stages of education was higher in 2015 than 2010 (figure 17b). Reasons for that include the increasing involvement of school-age males in income-generating activities. Young males belonging to this age group usually bear the burden if the family head is absent or unable to work. That is particularly true in times of conflict, when older males are obliged to carry out military service. A growing number of university-age males, compared with 2013, were either caught up in the fighting or had left the country in 2015.

Figure 17: Education (percentages)

A: Total enrolment in primary education

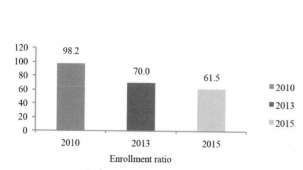

B: Female to male enrolment ratios

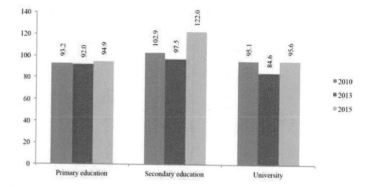

Source: ESCWA calculations based on data from the Syrian Ministry of Education, the Central Bureau of Statistics and SCPR.

The conflict has also had an impact on literacy. The national literacy rate of persons aged between 15 and 24 years fell only slightly between 2010 and 2013, from 94.9 per cent to 94.6 per cent. It has since dropped to 91.2 per cent, meaning that around 360,000 young Syrians are illiterate.[31]

1.3.5   HEALTH

The health sector has been especially hard hit, given that combatants consider its infrastructure and personnel to be legitimate targets. Shortages of medicines, spare parts, electrical power and trained staff have hampered the work of those facilities that have managed to continue working.

Almost half of the total 493 hospitals in the country in 2010 have been directly impacted in the five years of fighting. In 2015, 170 hospitals (34 per cent) were out of service and 69 (14 per cent) were only partially functioning.

One third (165) of the country's hospitals (88 per cent of them private) had been destroyed by 2015, and a further 11 per cent had been partially damaged. Repairing many of them was out of the question, since 119 of the destroyed or damaged hospitals were inaccessible and another 59 hard to reach (figure 18).

Figure 18: Operational public and private hospitals, 2015

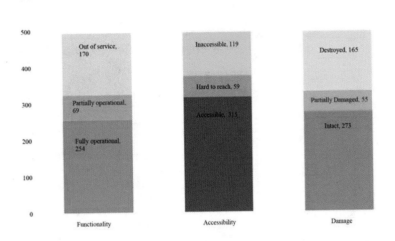

Source: Data from the Syrian Ministry of Health.

The deliberate targeting of doctors and pharmacists has forced many to flee the country, at a higher rate than that of the average population. As a result, the number of persons per doctor in the country rose from 661 in 2010 to 1,442 in 2015,[32] and per pharmacist from 1,246 to 1,789. Although public expenditure on health as a percentage of GDP has increased nominally from 1.8 per cent in 2010 to an average of 2 per cent during the crisis, the huge contraction in GDP means spending has fallen in real terms.[33]

The decline of healthcare services is reflected in steadily worsening health indicators since 2011. The net death rate, for instance, rose from 3.7 per thousand in 2010 to 10.9 per thousand in 2015, and reached 12.4 per thousand or more in governorates hardest hit by fighting (Aleppo, Dara, Deir el-Zor, Idlib and rural Damascus).[34] Maternal mortality rose from 56 per 100,000 live births in 2010 to 63.9 in 2015 (figure 19). Under-5 and infant mortality rates also rose over the same period, from 21.4 to 25.9 and 17.9 to 23.7 per thousand respectively.

Figure 19: Selected health indicators, 2010-2015

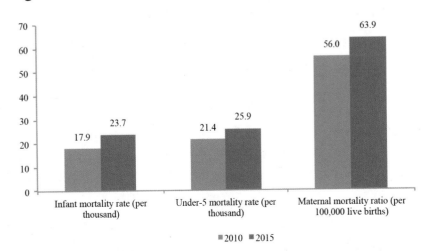

Sources: Data from the Syrian Ministry of Health and a population survey conducted by the Central Bureau of Statistics in 2014.

The rate of child immunization, which was close to 100 per cent across the country prior to the conflict, fell to an average of 75.2 per cent in 2014. However, there are large discrepancies between governorates: immunization rates in Aleppo, Al-Hasakeh and Quneitra were even lower, at 32.9 per cent, 66.8 per cent, and 70.2 per cent respectively. Consequently, diseases such as tuberculosis and measles began to spread widely.

Some diseases that had been eradicated prior to the conflict, such as polio, reappeared. In spite of tremendous efforts by the World Health Organization (WHO), UNICEF, the Syrian Ministry of Health and civil society organizations to confront this dire situation, some areas have remained out of immunization coverage. For instance, the indicator of 1-year-old children immunized against measles was 61.3 per cent in 2015, according to the Ministry of Health and UNICEF.

1.3.6   ACCESS TO WATER AND SANITATION

Housing services have deteriorated across the country since the conflict began, even in relatively secure areas, thus contributing to make the lives of many still more miserable. Syria was considered a water-poor country even before the crisis, with the share of drinking water per capita dropping from 91 cubic meters in 2001 to 72 cubic meters in 2011, although the proportion of population with access to safe drinking water increased from 86 per cent to 89.7 per cent over the same period. That figure fell slightly to 84 per cent by 2015. More seriously, the share of drinking water per capita has dropped dramatically to only 48 cubic meters.

That is a direct result of widespread damage to water infrastructure. According to the Syrian General Establishment for Drinking Water and Waste Disposal, loss of drinking water due to damaged pumps and pipelines reached 49 per cent of potential supply in 2015.

The sanitation picture is equally bleak. Prior to the conflict, 98.6 per cent of the population (in some cities the figure was 100 per cent) had access to improved sanitation facilities. According to the General Establishment for Drinking Water and Waste Disposal, that figure had fallen to 72 per cent by 2015. The proportion of the population benefiting from wastewater treatment stations fell from 52 per cent in 2010 to 9 per cent in 2015, largely as a result of inaccessibility and shrinking financial resources available for investment in wastewater treatment.

THE INTERNATIONAL PERSPECTIVE
WHAT CAN WE DO ?

The former United Nations envoy to Syria, Mr. Kofi Annan, launched the first international initiative for a political solution to the conflict in June 2012. It was followed by the Geneva II Conference on Syria in 2014 and more talks in 2016. In the meantime, an international coalition of Western countries and the Russian Federation launched separate military air campaigns in the country, each with different goals. A political solution will ultimately depend, at least in part, on those external powers. A flicker of hope came with a ceasefire declared at the end of February 2016, based on Security Council resolution 2254 (2015) and negotiated by the International Syria Support Group, in which regional and world powers have a presence. That paved the way for a new round of peace talks in Geneva in March 2016, but the political questions discussed there are beyond the scope of this paper. In this section, we will carry out socioeconomic analysis and examine policy options for the European Union (EU) and, in broader terms, the wider international community.

2.1 EUROPE

Relations between the EU and Syria prior to the war were largely governed by the 1977 Cooperation Agreement (as amended in 1986 and 1994), which mainly covers trade issues, such as duty free access to the EU market and assistance for production and economic infrastructure in Syria.[35] Only in the past few years did humanitarian issues come to the fore.

The EU was traditionally Syria's largest trading partner. Even in 2012, it was still that country's fourth most important trading partner after Iraq, Saudi Arabia and the United Arab Emirates.[36] In recent years China, Turkey and the Russian Federation have been gaining prominence. Syria is a member State of the Union for the Mediterranean. Its suspension from the European Neighbourhood Policy in 2011 because of "the ongoing repression in Syria and the unacceptable violence used by the military and security forces against peaceful protestors" dampened economic cooperation between the EU and Syria.[37]

More unilateral measures (economic sanctions and restrictions) followed. They included an EU ban on the import of crude oil and petroleum products from Syria, restrictions on exports from the EU of equipment used in the oil and gas and telecoms industries and a ban on the export of luxury goods. Assets linked to entities and people close to the Syrian regime were also frozen. As a result, trade with Syria shrank substantially. Between 2012 and 2013, for instance, imports from Syria to the EU dropped by 53 per cent and exports to Syria by 36 per cent.[38]

The conflict in Syria has caused the world's greatest humanitarian crisis since the Second World War and the EU with its member States have mobilized more than €5 billion in human-itarian aid to Syrians in Syria and neighbouring countries. A further €9 billion was pledged at the Supporting Syria and the Region conference, held in London in February 2016.[39] At that conference, the Secretary-General of the United Nations, Mr. Ban Ki-moon, outlined three main objectives for 2016: to raise $7 billion in immediate humanitarian aid, mobilize long-term support and protect civilians.[40] The largest obstacle to the provision of humanitarian aid to people in Syria is the lack of access to the affected areas, whether under the control of Government or opposition forces. The international community is working to negotiate ceasefires, like the one declared in late February 2016, and the opening of humanitarian corridors. The Humanitarian Aid and Civil Protection department (ECHO) of the European Commission needs to work with all stakeholders in order to establish where aid is most urgently required.

Migration flows within and out of the Arab region include regular and irregular labour migration, forced migration and mixed migration flows. Regular and irregular labour migrants look for better employment opportunities, within the region and beyond. Forced migrants flee conflict, persecution or severe breakdowns in public order. Finally, mixed migration flows of people crossing borders irregularly include forced and voluntary migrants motivated by a mixture of the above and other reasons.[41] In this part of the report, reference is made to mixed migration, refugees and migrants. Where data permit, we concentrate discussion on refugees or asylum-seekers. In other cases, we refer to migration in general which, in the eyes of the public and in the light of current events, is often associated with forced migration and with people from Syria, in particular, but also with people from other countries.

The following subsections look at support to the neighbouring countries carrying the main burden of the spillover from the conflict in Syria, and the complex issue of mixed migration flows to and within Europe. Discussion concentrates on the latter, as it is the issue over which, in terms of policy, the EU and its member countries have the most control.

2.1.1 EU SOCIOECONOMIC COOPERATION WITH SYRIA'S NEIGHBOURS

The most pressing issue for neighbouring countries, especially Jordan, Lebanon and Turkey (but also Egypt and Iraq), is how to create suitable living conditions for refugees, beyond mere shelter. That means providing access to health facilities, education for children, and work opportunities for breadwinners. Turkey hosts more than 2.7 million Syrian refugees (the most in absolute terms), followed by Lebanon with more than 1 million (by far the most in terms of share of population) and Jordan with almost 700,000. Around 10 per cent of the refugees live in camps and the rest in urban, peri-urban and rural areas.[42] Financial assistance provided by the EU and its member countries is therefore crucial.

In Lebanon, there are no official camps and refugees live in poor conditions. The EU therefore provides assistance with shelter for more than 125,000 refugees, along with other humanitarian assistance. More than 80 per cent of refugees in Jordan live in urban areas and EU aid is channelled through cash transfers and investment in facilities, in particular for health care and to meet the needs of children, in the Za'atari and Azraq refugee camps.

In Turkey, EU assistance, in particular for refugees living outside camps, covers access to health care, education for children, protection, and food and emergency items. In early 2016, the member countries of the EU agreed on how to finance its €3 billion refugee facility for Turkey. Initially, the EU pledged €55 million to address the immediate education needs of Syrian school children in Turkey and €40 million in humanitarian aid through the World Food Programme (WFP).[43]

Since December 2014, most non-humanitarian aid for Syria's neighbouring countries from the EU and member countries has gone through the EU Regional Trust Fund in Response to the Syrian Crisis, also known as the Madad Fund. It merges various EU financial instruments and contributions from member States "into one single flexible and quick mechanism" and "primarily addresses longer term resilience needs of Syrian refugees in neighbouring countries and host communities".[44]

The 3RP: Regional Refugee and Resilience Plan, launched by the Office of the United Nations High Commissioner for Refugees (UNCHR) and the United Nations Development Programme (UNDP) and owned by the five affected neighbouring countries (Egypt, Iraq, Jordan, Lebanon and Turkey), is a regionally coordinated inclusive model for delivering an effective and coordinated response with two parts, a refugee component and resilience component.[45] The 2016-2017 3RP includes more than 200 partners and appeals for $5.78 billion for the total programme response of Governments, United Nations agencies, intergovernmental organizations and NGOs.[46] The financial support to host countries, host communities and refugees, especially through the 3RP, is crucial but insufficient, especially when the resilience component is underfunded. After the most basic needs such as shelter, health care, food and water are met (and in many cases they have yet to be met), there is a need to provide education for children and productive employment for the working members of families. Around half of the refugees are children aged up to 17, while the rest (apart from around 3 per cent of elderly people aged 60 or more) are in their productive years. It is important that routines, in which children go to school (however improvised) and the working members of the family go to work, be established, wherever the refugees are housed.

In spite of the efforts of the EU Children for Peace initiative, which is active in Turkey,[47] and the No Lost Generation initiative, launched by UNICEF in 2013 to mitigate the impact of the Syria crisis on children, youth and adolescents through education, protection and adolescent and youth engagement (active in six countries),[48] many young people have yet to be reached. More than 60 per cent of young Syrian refugees in Turkey, almost half of those in Lebanon and more than 15 per cent in Jordan do not attend school. Participants in the February 2016 Supporting Syria and the Region conference committed themselves to working to enrol refugee children in Jordan, Lebanon and Turkey in school and to increase access to learning opportunities for children inside Syria.

Additional difficulties include lack of access to education above the primary level and, consequently, very low enrolment rates for secondary and, even more so, tertiary education (1 per cent of Syrians in Turkey, 6 per cent in Lebanon and 8 per cent in Jordan in 2014, compared with 20 per cent in pre-crisis Syria). Work needs to be done to discourage refugee families from sending younger male children to work, a common occurrence. The EU, with its world-class open secondary and tertiary education systems, could lead the way on this issue by providing targeted technical and financial assistance. Funds donated to mitigate the consequences of the conflict in 2015 fell 43 per cent short of the United Nations target.[49] As the closest most developed neighbourhood to the conflict area, the EU could seize the opportunity to fund education initiatives.

Employment for working age refugees is another conundrum. In most countries, refugees do not have the option of working legally. In Lebanon, refugees must sign a pledge upon renewal of their residency status to the effect that they will not work. In Jordan, refugees working illegally risk being returned to camps.[50] The lack of comprehensive national refugee legislation and policies on the rights and protection of vulnerable workers (especially refugees or asylum-seekers, both without work permits) makes them more susceptible to abusive practices by employers in the informal economy and becomes an added incentive to undertake the dangerous journey to Europe.

Under international pressure, attitudes appear to be changing. In early 2016, Turkey indicated that it would grant Syrian refugees who had been in the country for at least six months the right to apply for work permits in the province where they had first registered, and that they would be entitled to receive at least the minimum wage.[51] Jordan indicated that, in return $1.6 billion in aid over three years to support education, health care and job creation for refugees and Jordanians, it might grant 150,000 work permits for refugees in the coming years.[52] The EU could contribute with mechanisms to facilitate trade and capital flows between it and the host countries, and other compensatory measures for host countries that cooperate on improving work opportunities for refugees.

Refugees, host communities and the private sector could also ultimately benefit from creating employment opportunities in the communities in which they live. Syrian refugees have brought with them human capital and skills that could be put to use for mutual benefit. Such an approach would also counter the potential for political and religious radicalization of idle young refugees. Light manufacturing facilities could be set up in special industrial zones near areas densely populated by refugees, such as refugee camps. Such pockets of employment and productivity would not only benefit refugees, who would thus be able to support their families with dignity and legally contribute to society, but would also serve business interests. Such projects could eventually incorporate host country nationals too, and serve as an incubator for post-conflict recovery in Syria.

A potential example of this is the 2,100-ha King Hussein Bin Talal Development Area near Za'atari camp (which houses around 80,000 Syrian refugees) and the city of Mafraq in Jordan.[53] With its transport connections, logistical and hosting capacity, and regional markets exceeding 300 million people, it has enormous potential. At present it is operating at 10 per cent of capacity and is plagued by the lack of price competitive labour. With the right regulations, the zone could be a safe haven for Syrian businesses no longer able to operate in Syria, and for EU companies willing to relocate. The EU could set up a pilot project to coordinate between European businesses and the Jordanian authorities, offering the former concessional finance, price competitive (refugee) labour and privileged market access for regional companies setting up in the free zone.[54]

The light manufacturing facilities could employ Syrian refugees and Jordanian nationals, and be further attracted to the area by a simple, fast-tracked administration governed by Jordanian regulations. Jordan would benefit not only from the provision of work opportunities to refugees and Jordanians, but from the adding of new sectors to the real economy and tax revenues. It would be in the interests of the EU to promote and fund such a model, which by opening up possible livelihoods for refugees in their present host communities would also dampen their enthusiasm for attempting to reach Europe irregularly.

Financing for employment-generating projects can come from other sources as well. Arab countries with highly restrictive migration and asylum policies and ample fiscal space historically and in the medium term (albeit dependent on the price of crude oil), could team up with the EU in this endeavour and contribute to making the lives of

refugees better in host countries. Even more so, countries with a relative abundance of land or labour but a relative lack of technical expertise (such as the Sudan) could be interested in accepting refugees (as part of broader resettlement efforts described below) with the required technical skills for agricultural or manufacturing projects, supported by internationally financed job creation programmes. In the Arab region in particular, projects of this sort, linking fiscally more constrained with other less constrained countries, could go a long way to contributing to improving the situation of refugees and helping host countries.

Resettlement of refugees from an asylum country to another State that has agreed to admit them could represent a durable solution for the millions of Syrian refugees in camps. Only 28 countries currently participate in UNHCR resettlement efforts (in general, for all refugees). The United States is the world's top resettlement country, and Australia, Canada and the Nordic countries also provide a sizeable number of places every year. In 2014, the main beneficiaries of UNHCR-facilitated resettlement programmes were refugees from Syria.[55] These efforts can, and should, go further, and should not be unevenly focused on Europe or the EU. Nevertheless, the EU, with people waiting at the borders of its member States or already inside the Union, can do much to help.

2.1.2 MIXED MIGRATION FLOWS AND THE EUROPEAN UNION

The issue of mixed migration flows (refugees and migrants) heading for Europe has been the subject of heated political debate and media attention. The situation has been marked by a tendency to exaggerate the scale of the problem, a belated and uncoordinated response by the EU, its member States and other European countries, and a tendency to downplay the obligations of States under international refugee law (notably the 1951 Refugee Convention and its 1967 Protocol, and customary international law) and the positive economic potential in accepting refugees and migrants. In any event, this section deals primarily with labour market inclusion and social integration.

About half of the pre-war population of Syria has been displaced by the war, 6.6 million internally. Around 4.6 million have sought refuge in neighbouring countries and fewer than 1 million sought refuge in Europe (EU and the Balkans) between April 2011 and January 2016.[56] In relative terms, refugees in Turkey, Jordan and Lebanon represent 3.3 per cent, 10.7 per cent and 25 per cent of the population respectively. Those who have so far arrived in Europe represent 0.2 per cent of the population of the EU.

In recent years and up to 2015, Europe had not experienced large surges in irregular migration flows. In early 2016, nearly 2000 migrants and refugees were arriving in Europe daily, 10 times the average for the previous year.[57] Public opinion polls in 2015 suggested that immigration (often associated by the public with the more specific cases of refugees and asylum-seekers) had become the prime source of concern for 58 per cent of people in the EU (as much as 79 per cent in Estonia, and 76 per cent each in the Czech Republic, Denmark and Germany), ahead of terrorism (25 per cent) and the economy (21 per cent).[58]

European States that are parties to the 1951 Convention Relating to the Status of Refugees and its 1967 Protocol have a duty to accept refugees. One could also argue that European colonial involvement in the Arab region, particularly after the First World War, contributed in no small measure to the region's current problems. The historically special relationship that certain European powers have maintained with the region should be reflected in a willingness to welcome refugees and migrants in such difficult times. It is worth remembering that in the twentieth century it was often Europeans migrating to safer and more prosperous regions in the aftermath of the two world wars, during the Cold War and as a result of the disintegration of the former Yugoslavia.

The flow of forced migrants from Syria to Europe is neither unprecedented in historical terms nor large in terms of absolute or relative numbers. With some exceptions, such as the stance taken by Germany, reactions in Europe to the matter by politicians and the public have often been less than welcoming, even calling into question the future of the Schengen area, which governs the free movement of people within much of the EU and some non-EU members. The response of the EU to the flows of irregular migrants and refugees has been erratic. In spite of plans to establish 11 "hot spots" in Italy and Greece, the usual entry points of irregular migrants to the EU, for registration and status determination, only three, two in Italy and one in Greece, were operational in early 2016.[59] Quota schemes for the redistribution of 160,000 refugees across the member States in 2016 and 2017 have yet to be implemented and are opposed by East European States.

Although member States agreed in principle in 2015 to relocate more than 65,000 people from Greece and almost 40,000 from Italy, at the time of writing only 218 and 279, respectively, had in fact been moved. Moreover, 15 member countries had offered a total of just 1,081 places for refugees from Greece, and 966 from Italy.[61]

Within the EU, apart from reintroducing border controls and physical coercion, there is no apparent mechanism to oblige refugees and migrants to stay in a given location within the Schengen free movement area, once they enter it irregularly. The free movement system has thus effectively been suspended by Austria, Denmark, France, Germany, Norway and Sweden), some of which are among the desired final destinations of many refugees and migrants. They are also toughening regulations governing asylum and the right to residence.[62] In early 2016, the European Commission underscored the need for EU member States to tackle the migration crisis with common measures.

In February 2016, the European Commission issued a communication on migration in which it called on member countries of the European Union to commit to:

• "The urgent completion of the set-up of hotspots in Greece and Italy to ensure the registration of and support to migrants and refugees in line with the principle that no one should arrive in the EU without having been properly registered and fingerprinted, with dedicated EU support to secure increased reception capacity and fully functioning asylum and return procedures;

• The end of the 'wave-through' approach and an enforced insistence on the application of EU rules on asylum and border management;

• A major acceleration of the agreed relocation scheme to alleviate pressure from Italy and Greece;

• A stronger and more coherent use of the provisions allowing the return of asylum-seekers to safe third countries;

• Implementation of the agreed approach for better cooperation and coordination between countries along the Western Balkans route;

• A major stepping-up of all efforts to ensure effective returns and readmission and to address the root causes of migration by maximizing all forms of leverage, including trade preferences and development, to secure third countries' commitment to concrete outcomes;

• Driving forward the actions under: the EU-Turkey Joint Action Plan to stem the flows from Turkey; and rapid implementation of projects under the Facility for Refugees in Turkey;

• Stronger external border controls, by agreeing the European Border and Coast Guard at the latest by June, if not earlier, and by making it operational during the summer;

• Supporting the basic needs of the most vulnerable migrants and refugees, and in particular children;

• Stepping up the capacity for the EU to provide humanitarian assistance to third countries, and establishment of a capacity to provide humanitarian assistance within the EU, to support countries facing large numbers of refugees and migrants;

• Stepping up EU support to Syrian refugees, including opening up legal pathways through resettlement and endorsement of the voluntary humanitarian admission scheme with Turkey, as recommended by the Commission on 15 December 2015."

Source: European Commission, 2016a

The policy option of relocating refugees already in Europe, or accepting more from Jordan, Lebanon and Turkey, gets little attention, possibly because of misconceptions about the long-term costs (in economic and social terms) and potential benefits of immigration in general.

It is commonly perceived that accepting refugees entails a heavy financial burden for host countries, as argued before in the case of Syria's neighbours. However, there is a big difference in the absolute and relative size of the mixed migration flows to Syria's neighbours and to Europe, and in the development level, fiscal space and capacity to deal with relatively unexpected surges of immigration (be it regular or irregular).

For instance, the 2013 International Migration Outlook, published by the Organisation for Economic Cooperation and Development (OECD), concluded that, in the case of 27 rich countries, immigration over the previous 50 years had presented "neither a significant gain nor drain for the public purse". Moreover, spending on refugees can stimulate domestic demand.[63] The German Institute for Economic Research (DIW Berlin) has concluded that successful integration of refugees brings net benefits to the economy within four to five years under an optimistic, and 10 years under a pessimistic, scenario: "Even if only some of the refugees are successfully integrated into the labour market, the investment pays off."[64]

As for the effects on the labour market, "studies conclude that immigration's effects on the wages and employment of native workers are either small or non-existent",[65] with some pressure on low value-added jobs and lowest wages.[66] Some studies show that, as in the case of Denmark, allowing low-skilled immigrants access to the labour market has encouraged less educated nationals to upgrade their skills and has led to wage increases, especially for younger and less experienced workers.[67]

A study of social contributions and spending in Sweden, where refugees represent 5.1 per cent of the total population, shows that they account for a commensurate 5.6 per cent of public spending. It suggests that the country's generous refugee welfare policy, with a redistribution from nationals to refugees costing around 1.35 per cent of GDP, is not an overly heavy economic burden. That is especially noteworthy given the generous welfare system for people without employment history and the fact that the Swedish labour market, with few simple jobs, is difficult for refugees without the appropriate schooling and language skills to enter.[68]

The European Commission predicts that the employment of refugees could add 0.2 or 0.3 percentage points to projected GDP in the EU for 2020.[69] The key is rapid inclusion of refugees in to the labour market. Employment will help them with social integration, make it easier to afford decent housing, and thereby diminish their reliance on social transfer, and allow them to pay taxes, contribute to social security and stimulate the economy through consumer spending.

A quarter of Europeans is expected to be over 60 years of age by 2020, increasing pressure on pension, social security and health systems.[70] EU countries can benefit from the arrival of Syrian refugees, 45 per cent of whom are of working age (18-59) to secure high living standards in the future. "Back-of-the-envelope" calculations show that, for instance, real GDP in Nordic countries could be about 2.5 per cent higher by 2020 than it would be if immigration to those countries ceased.[71] The average EU fertility rate of 1.55 per cent (lower still in Poland, Portugal and Spain), below the rate of 2.1 needed to maintain population constant, is exacerbating the unfavourable worker to pension ratio. That perhaps explains why Spain has dropped opposition to the quota relocation scheme for refugees.[72] The EU needs more than just highly skilled, university-educated labour.

Many businesses rely on trained individuals with minimal to moderate qualifications. Indeed, a recent study by the International Labour Organization (ILO) showed that a growing problem in at least half of the countries in Europe is over-education, and not under-education.[73] Germany, for instance, needs more than half a million immigrants per year to offset that trend.[74] Its "early intervention" project aims to incorporate migrants and refugees into the labour market quickly by determining what competencies are needed and where. In addition, "talent scouts" match well-trained refugees with the appropriate businesses.[75]

Early inclusion of refugees in the job market is thus one of the best investments the EU can make and countries with economic foresight will accept more rather than fewer refugees. A series of potential policy options appeared in a paper published by UNHCR in 2013, which makes the following policy recommendations for labour market integration:[76]

• Mechanisms for researching the needs of refugees and employers, and adapting policy to different subgroups of refugees (State Refugee Coordinator of Colorado)

• Individualized employment plans (two-year introductory programme in Denmark)

• Outreach and partnering with employers/the private sector, with a view to matching workers with employer needs and creating a positive community culture inclined to hire refugees (Extended Network of Institutions for the Reception and Integration of Refugees and Asylum Seekers in Portugal)

• Subsidized, unsubsidized or unpaid work programmes for initial placements with potential employers (Swedish Public Employment Service)

• Vocationally-focused language courses with integrated work experience (language apprenticeships in Norway, in which refugees spend two days per week at a workplace gaining work experience and learning work-related vocabulary)

• Assistance with recertification

• Partnering with the broader community to foster social support and networks (WOMENTO mentoring project for women in Finland)

• Microenterprise and alternative employment programmes (United States Central Office of Refugee Resettlement offers two microenterprise development programmes)

Laws and regulations should be amended in EU member countries in order to allow refugees, asylum-seekers and other immigrants who are not threatened with immediate relocation or deportation the possibility of receiving temporary work permits and to enrol in subsidized courses, such as on the local language, while their status is pending. Possible incentives for private-sector employers to take on migrant labour could include tax breaks and subsidies for employers, and temporary, targeted exemptions from the payment of minimum wages.[77]

The real migration issue in the EU is social rather than economic. Well designed social integration programmes are therefore crucial. Displacement is generally not short-term. The average duration of residence abroad for refugees has increased from nine years in 1993 to nearly 20 years today.[78]

Taking measures to discourage refugees and other irregular migrants from embarking on the dangerous journey to Europe by whatever route and toughening asylum procedures will not dissuade them from making the attempt, as research has shown.[79] In addition to assistance for refugees living in neighbouring countries, paths are needed to allow refugees to reach the EU legally, for instance via resettlement.

In December 2015, the European Commission recommended the introduction of a voluntary humanitarian admission scheme for Syrian refugees in Turkey, but it has yet to be activated.[80] More such options should be explored, to save refugees the perilous journey in the hands of people smugglers and to give the EU and other European States greater control over refugee flows.

The 11 hot spots planned for Italy and Greece, when all are operational, should help to prevent duplication of registration processes and facilitate the relocation of refugees and their inclusion in labour markets, so long as they are provided with temporary residence permits pending decisions on their asylum applications. In order to take pressure off Greece and Italy and allow refugees to get on with their lives in their final destination, the proposed quota resettlement scheme must be fully functional.[81] Decisions to grant asylum should be recognized across the EU and not just in the country where the decision is taken, thereby facilitating resettlement efforts within the EU.

Security concerns have been raised in Europe with regard to the current wave of irregular migrants. While the presence of extremists among those entering Europe cannot be discounted, the main long-term concern is to avoid the mistakes of the past. Earlier waves of migrants faced under-employment and exclusion, which created fertile ground for extremist ideologies and violence.

The violence in Europe in the past decade, including the recent attacks in Paris and Brussels, has been overwhelmingly the work of young people born in Europe and radicalized by their shunned communities. Social exclusion, a lack of investment, hands-off policies and poor socioeconomic integration have all contributed. That underlines the need for well designed economic and social programmes for refugees and migrants, especially after resettlement.

The authorities in host countries should provide asylum-seekers with access to quality health-care services, without adversely affecting the broader population. Almost half of the Syrian asylum-seekers entering Europe are young people up to 18 years old who need access to good quality education at all levels, without discrimination and taking into account language and cultural challenges.

Four key areas for the integration of resettled refugees are discussed in a study published by the European Parliament in 2013:

• Secure legal status with the possibility of eventually receiving citizenship (such as in the Czech Republic, France, Ireland, Sweden and the United Kingdom)

• Individualized support, pre-departure orientation programmes and the involvement of refugee community organizations in resettlement (the Netherlands provides a six-day cultural and language orientation training programme)

• Improved coordination, for instance between NGOs and local authorities, in areas such as pre-arrival planning, language training, phasing into mainstream services and assistance with job market entry (Denmark offers pre- and post-arrival language training)

• Efforts to strengthen host communities through advance planning, information meetings, regular (rather than ad hoc) resettlement, and sustained funding (in Sweden, information meetings are held by the receiving municipalities with NGOs and churches).[82]

The same study recommended the application of common EU criteria to promote and monitor the integration of refugees; results-driven resettlement financing by the European Refugee Fund; greater cooperation between States, NGOs and international organizations; and publication by the European Commission of guidelines on the reception and integration of resettled refugees.

2.2 UNILATERAL MEASURES AND UNINTENDED HUMANITARIAN CONSEQUENCES

As the situation in Syria has deteriorated, a complex array of sanctions has been imposed by the EU, the League of Arab States, the United States and various other countries. They typically target the Government of Syria, and entities and individuals deemed to have engaged in violence and/or human rights abuses. For instance, the EU has placed sanctions on more than 200 persons and 70 entities.[83]

Prohibitions are wide-ranging and vary considerably. EU sanctions and export controls include: asset freezes; restrictions on services European banks may offer in Syria; a prohibition on the export of certain "dual use" goods to Syria; and requirements to obtain prior authorisation in certain situations. In addition, broad ranging bans and prohibitions exist in respect of the electricity, oil and gas sectors, specifically related to: technical and financial assistance; construction/investment in new electricity power plants in Syria; and the export of key equipment and technology for the oil and gas industry.[84]

Sanctions and export control regulations imposed by the United States are still more restrictive and broadly prohibit the involvement of any "United States person" (individual or entity under United States law) in transactions involving Syria. Hence, no United States bank (or bank transmitting United States dollar payments) can process transactions involving Syria, unless licensed to do so. In addition, United States persons may not facilitate transactions by non-United States persons in Syria. Because the United States considers Syria to be a State sponsor of terrorism, the export to Syria of almost all items with a United States origin is banned. The ban includes foreign-produced items in which United States content accounts for 10 per cent or more of the value of the finished product.[85] The loss of infrastructure, including power stations, hospitals, water and fuel installations in Syria, has fuelled the need for the very types of investment, services, technology and dual use goods that are subject to sanctions. Moreover, the effectiveness of sanctions is disputed. Their chances of success, according to one study, are as much as twice as high against a democracy as against an authoritarian regime.[86]

2.2.1 USE OF SANCTIONS

Governments adopting sanctions attempt to minimize their impact on the civilian population and those carrying out legitimate activities in or with the country, and seek not to obstruct, for example, the export of medicines, food supplies or other humanitarian goods. However, sanctions against Syria have prevented the import of specialized therapeutic drugs, raw materials needed to produce drugs, specialized medical equipment and spare parts.[87]

The negative impact of sanctions, especially when they consist of generalized coercive measures, on the general population is a source of great concern. The sanctions imposed on Iraq by the United Nations Security Council from 1990 to 2003 are a case in point.

UNICEF estimated that, by the end of the first decade of sanctions, the under-5 and infant mortality rates had doubled, leading to half a million more deaths between 1990 and 1998 than would have occurred had the trend of falling mortality rates prior to the sanctions remained steady.[88] The sanctions led to a scarcity of medical supplies, high rates of malnutrition and the spread of diseases due to a lack of clean water.[89]

2.2.2 OBSTACLES TO THE DELIVERY OF HUMANITARIAN AID

Even in those cases where sanctions programmes provide exemptions for the export of humanitarian goods, the procedures involved can be opaque, unpredictable and time-consuming, and frequently require costly legal advice.[90]

The practicalities involved in navigating permissions procedures is often far removed from the policy commitment of limiting the impact of sanctions on civilian populations and humanitarian aid providers. The latter are often discouraged from applying to use United States goods and services, even if they are subject to "favourable licensing policies". Further frustration stems from the duplication of bureaucratic licensing procedures between, for instance, the United States and the EU. In some cases, NGOs and other aid providers simply do not seek permission, either due to a lack of knowledge or fear that slow response time will create missed opportunities.

Moreover, in instances where no licence is required, the fear that goods or finances could be diverted to targeted individuals or entities has created a "chilling effect", whereby financial institutions and exporters go beyond the requirements of the sanctions in order to avoid the risk of violating sanctions.

A review by the US law firm, Hughes Hubbard & Reed LLP, highlights the difficulties faced by those running humanitarian programmes for Syria. US export control regulations do not permit either the United Nations or NGOs to export the full range of items necessary for basic human needs without specific licences. The general US licence covering the activities of NGOs does not extend to private contractors engaged by NGOs. The US regulations do not allow the export of medical devices without a licence, and the licence does not apply to software or software updates required to operate such devices.[91]

Prior to the conflict, Syria was relatively self-sufficient in domestically produced medicines. The few factories still operating after five years of war have major difficulties in procuring the raw materials required to manufacture medicines. Suppliers have become increasingly reluctant due to payment problems and their fears of being found in breach of sanctions.[92]

The electricity sector in Syria has been hit heavily by the conflict. Experts say that what is left of the grid is in dire need of critical servicing, modernization and standard maintenance.[93] That means providing spare parts, re-commissioning equipment and purchasing new technologies. Where external donors, in conjunction with the United Nations, have attempted to tackle such issues in the electricity and other sectors in areas of the country held either by the Government or by non-Government forces, they have come up against major sanctions-related obstacles.

They include the time taken to secure permits, exporter compliance costs (which lead many exporters to just "walk away"), and a blanket unwillingness to fund the supply of dual-use parts to Syria, all of which means that many critical programmes cannot be funded.

2.2.3 LACK OF BANKING CHANNELS TO SUPPORT HUMANITARIAN AID IN SYRIA

Even where it is possible to deliver humanitarian aid on the ground, sending funds and goods to Syria without violating sanctions or the regulations of neighbouring countries can be fraught with difficulty. The "strict liability" nature of the sanctions regime (whereby a person or entity may be penalized regardless of whether they were aware of committing a violation or not) and the threat of hefty fines for violations have led banks to refuse to process humanitarian aid transactions denominated in US dollars even when they are legal.[94]

As a result of the sanctions on Government-owned banks and the collapse of the banking system in areas not held by the Government, it has become extraordinarily difficult to carry out dollar or euro transactions in Syria.

The impossibility of making direct bank-to-bank payments into Syria means that funds must normally transit through neighbouring countries. International NGOs send donated funds to Iraq, Jordan, Lebanon and, above all, Turkey by bank transfer, either to their office or directly into the account of their implementing partner.[95] At this point, the formal banking relationship ends and the informal chain is activated. It is also here that the regulatory/ sanctions risk profile of such payments increases considerably.

However, even some of those payment routes are becoming more complicated. Transfers destined for Syria and sent to Lebanon face further hurdles under the US Hizballah International Financing Prevention Act of 2015, which punishes persons or institutions facilitating "significant transactions" with Hezbollah.

Since mid-2015, payments sent to Turkey have been affected by Law No. 6493, which requires payment service providers, including those offering remittance/*hawala* transfers, to obtain a licence. NGOs confirm that difficulties in moving funds have delayed and in some cases prevented the delivery of humanitarian assistance in Government and non-Government held areas.[96]

Banks view sanctions risks in the broader context of requirements to combat money-laundering, terrorist financing and corruption, and other factors such as beneficial ownership transparency. A prime concern is that humanitarian payments may be used to disguise the movement of funds to support – directly or indirectly – terrorist activity, or unwittingly be diverted from their intended use. In order to mitigate that risk, charities are expected to screen charity staff, partners, partner staff, banks, money agents and suppliers against counter-terrorism and sanctions lists. Completing such due diligence in the home country of the charity and for stable environment projects is relatively straightforward. It is much more complex in the field, especially in the high-risk fluid environments in which aid agencies are often required to work.

Standard setters (such as the Financial Action Task Force[97]), Governments and regulators need to work more closely together and accept that there is no fail-safe solution to transferring money into a conflict zone such as Syria.

There are lower and higher risk remittance corridors that should be assessed in order to establish which are acceptable and viable.[98] Without pragmatic responses, moving money into Syria is likely to become increasingly difficult.

2.2.4 MOVING TOWARDS NEEDS-DRIVEN HUMANITARIAN EXEMPTIONS FRAMEWORKS

Governments need to fine tune the implementation of sanctions and raise awareness about how they work among the wider community. A more pragmatic and permissive framework is needed to make the delivery of humanitarian aid viable. The exemptions framework used in cases such as that of the Islamic Republic of Iran is woefully inadequate in a country engulfed by civil war.

A coherent shared position across Governments, regulators, banks and NGOs is required to address possible sanctions violations and regulatory concerns and at the same time to prevent the devastating consequences that have arisen from sanctions in other conflict scenarios, such as the famine in Somalia in 2011.[99]

First, the United Nations and its representatives should be permitted to export humanitarian goods to Syria without a licence. At present, for instance, the US framework allows the United Nations to export only food and certain medicines to Syria without a licence. That falls far short of what is needed. The list of items than can be exported should also be broadened.

At the very least, the EU, United States and other Governments imposing sanctions should add a "favourable licensing policy" for requests made by the United Nations, its agencies and their representatives to provide humanitarian assistance. That would include the export to Syria of certain dual use items not on the "basic human needs" list, such as vehicles and heavy machinery for building shelter.

A network of vetted NGOs and their private contractors that would not need a licence to export humanitarian goods could be established, following the example of the United States Treasury with regard to the Sudan.[100] Such a move should also address the issue of moving funds in support of their work.

Enhanced permissions to allow the licence-free export of medical devices, and their related software, to Syria would go some way to filling the critical gap that has developed in Syrian hospitals. Where Governments require licences, expedited licence review systems should be set up. Guidance notes on when licences are needed and how best to obtain them should also be issued.

The EU and United States should work together to ensure that at least one reputable financial institution in Syria can be used for the inflow of humanitarian aid funds, perhaps by establishing partnerships with one or more foreign financial institutions operating in Syria that are not subject to sanctions.

An alternative could be to establish a new banking and oversight channel that could provide dedicated links to the international financial system and have the capacity to process United States dollar-denominated transactions. Indeed, deliberations have already begun on the possible creation of a coordinated multi-donor trust fund/development bank. In any event, the establishment of a secure financial corridor into Syria, in support of immediate post-conflict recovery and reconstruction, should be a priority.

Governments that have imposed sanctions should be planning for reconstruction in Syria. Past experience shows that the impact of sanctions lasts long after they have been lifted. Even in relatively stable situations, it can take up to two years before the private sector becomes confident enough to re-engage with the country that was under sanctions.[101]

Sanctioning Governments should also be planning ahead to have new export regulations ready for implementation when the time comes to support reconstruction in Syria. The goal would be to shorten the inevitable time lag between when events occur and regulations are promulgated. That is of critical importance, given the urgent need to repair Syrian oil and gas fields, infrastructure, medical facilities and the transport network.

THE WAY
FORWARD
IN SYRIA

A partial ceasefire went into effect in Syria on 27 February 2016, opening the way to negotiations between the Government and opposition groups and the hope of an agreement to resolve the conflict. We are already in a position to identify the guiding principles and key steps that should follow such an agreement in order to end the suffering of the Syrian people and ensure that it does not reoccur.

GUIDING PRINCIPLES

1 – INDIVISIBILITY

Over the past five years, various proposals have been put forward for dividing Syria into several autonomous States along sectarian or ethnic lines. All such entities would lack economic viability and lead to the displacement of parts of the population. The unhappy experience of Iraq is instructive in that regard. Syria should thus be treated as a single, indivisible entity in which all of its citizens, regardless of religion, sect or ethnicity, have equal rights and responsibilities. Various forms of administrative decentralization, however, could prove helpful, provided the Syrian people agreed to them.

2 – PRIORITIZATION

Post-war efforts must be concentrated in the first instance on those segments of the population that are living in the harshest of conditions. Many Syrians today not only suffer from poverty, but are also deprived of the very basic necessities of life, including nutrition, health care, adequate housing and access to water, and policymakers should address their needs first.

3 – RETURN OF SYRIANS TO SYRIA

Given the pressing needs of Syrians inside the country, there is a danger that the needs of Syrian refugees might be neglected. The conditions for their return home should be created as soon as possible.

4 – SAFETY AND SECURITY

Prior to March 2011, it was safe to wander the streets of Syrian cities and towns even late into the night. Today, Syrian citizens lack faith in the capacity of the authorities to guarantee basic security. As the Iraqi experience has shown, it is impossible to embark on sustainable reconstruction without security. A lack of safety would also dissuade those who left Syria from returning.

5 – RATIONAL POLICYMAKING

Policymakers need to resist kneejerk reactions in post-conflict reconstruction planning. Rebuilding needs to be carried out on rational grounds and in such a way as to avoid past errors, such as ignoring environmental impact, disregarding basic urban and regional planning needs, and marginalizing certain population groups. A vision of everything that Syria could be and everything that it could have avoided in the past should inform pragmatic reconstruction planning.[102]

6 – ORGANIZATIONAL INCLUSION

Another lesson learned in Iraq is that the dismantling of official bodies, many of them with a deeply rooted institutional legacy, should be avoided. Rather, they and entities outside Government control, including civil society groups that have emerged in the past five years, should be encouraged to contribute to the rebuilding of Syria. Movements and organizations, especially those deemed to be credible by the Government and opposition groups, should be allowed to work as bridges on the path to societal reconciliation.

7 – GRADUALISM

The level of destruction suffered by the country is such that rebuilding will take time. The failure to ignore that principle and the temptation to act hurriedly could lead to results that are neither sustainable nor effective. The following critical steps constitute the outline of a potential plan for gradual recovery:

CRITICAL STEPS

The aim of the National Agenda for the Future of Syria (NAFS) programme is to present national and regional stakeholders with viable solutions and practical scenarios that may serve as a foundation for rebuilding Syria. The programme was developed under the umbrella of ESCWA in conjunction with various partners in Syria in order to anticipate technical post-conflict challenges, especially in relation to their implications for regional development and stability.

1. Emergency response, relief and humanitarian aid: Temporary facilities will be needed to accommodate the displaced, returning refugees and people living in the harshest conditions. They will include temporary settlements, medical facilities, schools, power generators and storage facilities for food and water, and be managed by coordination committees.

2. Institutional reform: It will be critical to identify which institutions, including legislative bodies, the judicial system, the security forces, and the framework in which civil society operates, require reform and the nature of the reforms needed. The role of those institutions will be crucial to the process of rebuilding.

3. Reconciliation and transitional justice: Reconciliation committees should be established at the local and national levels, along with truth and transitional justice committees and compensation funds to address grievances pertaining to loss of property. The experience of lessons learned in countries such as South Africa will be invaluable.

4. Rehabilitation of physical and social infrastructure: Emphasis will need to be placed on guaranteeing the provision of water and electricity, improving housing, restoring transport networks, and repairing roads and urban infrastructure, and organizing the disposal of solid and liquid waste (including sewage, rubble and remnants of war).

5. Human development and improving the quality of life: The focus of this step will be on the prompt creation of income-generating activities, especially for people who lost their livelihoods as a result of the crisis and returning refugees. Special attention will need to be paid to the economic empowerment of women in view of the large number of households headed by women who have lost husbands or fathers to the war. There will be a demand for professional support to victims, especially children, of physical and psychological violence, and for rehabilitation facilities for the injured and disabled.

6. Governance initiatives: During the immediate post-war period, there will be a need to empower local governments (on the principle of local resources management) and focus on conflict resolution and the management of expectations. Special attention will have to be paid to defining and managing relations between the central Government and local authorities.

7. Social equality, inclusive development and growth: The financial foundations of the war economy will need to be dismantled and viable alternatives found for those affected. Tackling poverty will have to be a top priority.

8. Technical development and management of natural and environmental resources: The authorities will need to tap expertise and technologies capable of dealing with tasks arising from the massive level of destruction, including rubble recycling, the clearance of dangerous objects (including landmines), and tackling environmental hazards. Environmental principles and natural resources management will need to be considered in regional and urban planning.

9. Communications and information: Mechanisms will be needed to collect data systematically on quality of life, especially in areas most affected by the violence. Emphasis will be placed on the need for autonomous and credible media. Enhancing information and communications technologies in the country and unfettered access to data will be crucial.

10. Regional integration and international relations: An Arab Fund should be set up to support reconstruction in Syria and other countries affected by the crisis. Resources pledged by the international community for reconstruction need to be matched up with priority post-conflict tasks. There should be policy focus on lifting international sanctions, if still in place, especially those that clearly obstruct humanitarian aid and reconstruction efforts.

REFERENCES

Abu-Ismail, Khalid, and Heba El-Laithy (2009). Poverty and income distribution in Syria. Damascus: UNDP.

The Assessment Capacities Project (ACAPS) (2015). Syria crisis: scenarios, possible developments in Syria over the next 12 months. November. Available from http://acaps.org/img/documents/s-acaps-scenarios-syria-26-nov-2015.pdf.

Aiyar, Shekhar, and others (2016). The refugee surge in Europe: economic challenges. IMF Staff Discussion Note SDN/16/02.

Barker, Memphis (2015). "Four problems with Europe's refugee quota: it came at a cost, and a significant one." The Independent, 2 October 2015. Available from www.independent.co.uk/voices/four-problems-with-europes-refugee-quota-a6676841.html.

Barut, M. Jamal (2013). The First Syrian Congress 1919-1920. Tabayyun lil-Dirāsāt al-Fikrīyah wa-al-Thaqāfīyah, 1(3)8.

Betts, Alexander, and others (2014). Refugee Economies: Rethinking Popular Assumptions. Oxford: Refugee Studies Centre, University of Oxford. Available from www.rsc.ox.ac.uk/files/publications/other/refugee-econo-mies-2014.pdf.

British Bankers Association (2014a). Coordinated report on "de-risking" submitted to the Financial Action Task Force (FATF). October. London.

_____ (2014b). Presentation to annual sanctions conference on Myanmar. September. London.

Calamur, Krishnadev (2015). "The economic impact of the European refugee crisis", The Atlantic, 5 November. Available from www.theatlantic.com/international/archive/2015/11/economic-impact-european-refugee-crisis/414364.

Calì, Massimiliano and Samia Sekkarie (2015). Much ado about nothing? The economic impact of refugee 'invasions'. 16 September. Washington D.C.: Brookings. Available from www.brookings.edu/blogs/future-devel-opment/posts/2015/09/16-economic-impact-refugees-cali.

Checchi, Francesco and W. Courtland Robinson (2013). Mortality among populations of southern and central Somalia affected by severe food insecurity and famine during 2010-2012. May. Food and Agriculture Organi-zation (FAO) and USAID. Available from http://reliefweb.int/sites/reliefweb.int/files/resources/Somalia_Mortali-ty_Estimates_Final_Report_1May2013.pdf.

Chokshi, Niraj (2016) "The stunning acceleration of Europe's migration crisis, in one chart", The Washington Post, 10 February. Available from https://www.washingtonpost.com/news/worldviews/wp/2016/02/10/the-stun-ning-acceleration-of-europes-migration-crisis-in-one-chart/?tid=a_inl.

Collier, Paul (2015). Beyond The Boat People: Europe's Moral Duties To Refugees. July. Social Europe. Available from www.socialeurope.eu/2015/07/beyond-the-boat-people-europes-moral-duties-to-refugees.

Cook, Lorne (2016). "Refugee crisis: Six countries in Schengen now have border checks in place", The Inde-pendent, 4 January. Available from www.independent.co.uk/news/world/europe/refugee-crisis-six-countries-in-schengen-now-have-border-checks-in-place-a6796296.html.

Cook, B. I., and others (2016). "Spatiotemporal drought variability in the Mediterranean over the last 900 years". Journal of Geophysical Research: Atmospheres.

Council of the European Union (2011). Council Conclusions on Syria. Available from www.consilium.europa.eu/uedocs/cms_data/docs/pressdata/EN/foraff/122168.pdf.

_____ (2015). Syria: EU extends sanctions against the regime and its supporters by one year. Available from www.consilium.europa.eu/en/press/press-releases/2015/05/28-syria-sanctions.

Deeb, Kamal (2011). Tarikh Suriyah al-mu'asir min al-intidab ila sayf 2011 (History of Modern Syria from the French Mandate and until the Summer of 2011). Beirut: Dar al-Nahar.

De Freytas-Tamura, Kimiko and Milan Schreuer (2015). "Paris attacks: the violence, its victims and how the investigation unfolded", The New York Times, 15 November. Available from www.nytimes.com/live/paris-at-tacks-live-updates/belgium-doesnt-have-control-over-molenbeek-interior-minister-says.

De La Baume, Maia (2016). "Why the EU's refugee relocation policy is a flop", Politico, 6 january 2016. Available from: www.politico.eu/article/why-eu-refugee-relocation-policy-has-been-a-flop-frontex-easo-med.

Delegation of the European Union to Syria. European Syrian Cooperation Agreement. Available from http://eeas.europa.eu/delegations/syria/eu_syria/political_relations/agreements/index_en.htm.

Dettmer, Markus, Carolin Katschak and Georg Ruppert (2015). "Rx for Prosperity: German Companies See Refugees as Opportunity", Speigel Online, 27 August. Available from www.spiegel.de/international/germany/refugees-are-an-opportunity-for-the-german-economy-a-1050102.html.

Directorate General for Internal Policies (2013). Comparative study on the best practices for the integration of resettled refugees in the EU Member States. PE 474.393. Strasbourg: European Parliament. Available from http://www.resettlement.eu/sites/icmc.tttp.eu/files/EP%20study.pdf.

European Commission (2014). Population ageing in Europe Facts, implications and policies. Brussels.

_____ (2015a). Commission Recommendation of 15.12.2015 for a voluntary humanitarian admission scheme with Turkey. Brussels. Available from http://ec.europa.eu/dgs/home-affairs/what-we-do/policies/securing-eu-borders/legal-documents/docs/commission_recommendation_for_a_voluntary_humanitarian_admission_scheme_with_turkey_en.pdf.

_____ (2015b). Commission Staff working document Turkey 2015 Report. SWD(2015) 216. Brussels.

_____ (2015c). Progress report on the implementation of the hotspots in Greece. COM(2015) 678. Brussels. Available from http://ec.europa.eu/dgs/home-affairs/what-we-do/policies/securing-eu-borders/legal-documents/docs/communication_-_progress_report_on_the_implementation_of_the_hotspots_in_greece_en.pdf.

_____ (2015d). Press release: Commission presents recommendation for a voluntary humanitarian admission scheme with Turkey for refugees from Syria. 15 December. Brussels Available from http://europa.eu/rapid/press-release_IP-15-6330_en.htm.

_____ (2015e). European Economic Forecast. Institutional paper 011. November. Available from http://ec.europa.eu/economy_finance/publications/eeip/pdf/ip011_en.pdf.

_____ (2015f). Fact sheet: the European Union and Syria, 131018/01. 5 February. Brussels. Available from http://eeas.europa.eu/statements/docs/2013/131018_01_en.pdf.

_____ (2015g). Press release: European Commission makes progress on agenda on migration. 27 May. Brussels. Available from http://europa.eu/rapid/press-release_IP-15-5039_en.htm.

_____ (2015h). Refugee crisis: European Commission takes decisive action. 9 September. Brussels. Available from http://europa.eu/rapid/press-release_IP-15-5596_en.htm.

_____ (2015i). Public opinion in the European Union. Standard Eurobarometer 84. August. Brussels. Available from http://ec.europa.eu/COMMFrontOffice/PublicOpinion/index.cfm/ResultDoc/download/DocumentKy/70150.

_____ (2015j). Restrictive measures (sanctions) in force. Brussels. Available from http://eeas.europa.eu/cfsp/sanctions/docs/measures_en.pdf. Accessed on 1 November 2015.

_____ (2016a). The state of play of implementation of the priority actions under the European Agenda on Migration. 10 February. Brussels. Available from http://ec.europa.eu/dgs/home-affairs/what-we-do/policies/european-agenda-migration/proposal-implementation-package/docs/managing_the_refugee_crisis_state_of_play_20160210_en.pdf.

_____ (2016b). Humanitarian aid and civil protection. Syria crisis. ECHO Factsheet. Brussels. Available from http://ec.europa.eu/echo/files/aid/countries/factsheets/syria_en.pdf.

_____ (2016c). Fact sheet: EU support in response to the Syrian crisis. 5 February. Brussels. Available from http://europa.eu/rapid/press-release_MEMO-16-222_en.htm.

_____(2016d). Press release: EU announces first projects under the Facility for Refugees in Turkey: €95 million to be provided for immediate educational and humanitarian assistance. 4 March. Brussels. Available from http://europa.eu/rapid/press-release_IP-16-584_en.htm.

_____ (2016e). Press release: Implementing the European Agenda on Migration: Commission reports on progress in Greece, Italy and the Western Balkans. Available from http://europa.eu/rapid/press-release_IP-16-269_en.htm.

_____ (2016f). Syrian crisis (infographic). 4 February. Brussels. Available from http://ec.europa.eu/echo/sites/echo-site/files/infographic_syriancrisis_2016_en.pdf.

_____ (n.d.a). European schemes for relocation and resettlement. Brussels. Available from http://ec.europa.eu/dgs/home-affairs/what-we-do/policies/european-agenda-migration/background-information/docs/communication_on_the_european_agenda_on_migration_annex_en.pdf.

_____ (n.d.b). Trade: Syria. Brussels. Available from http://ec.europa.eu/trade/policy/countries-and-regions/countries/syria.

European Union (2015). EU children of peace. November. Available from http://ec.europa.eu/echo/files/aid/countries/factsheets/thematic/eu_children_of_peace_en.pdf.
European Union External Action (n.d.b). Sanctions policy. Brussels. Available from http://eeas.europa.eu/cfsp/sanctions/index_en.htm.

Financial Action Task Force (FATF) (n.d.) Available from www.fatf-gafi.org.

Fleming, Melissa (2015) "Six reasons why Syrians are fleeing to Europe in increasing numbers", The Guardian, 25 October. Available from www.theguardian.com/global-development-professionals-network/2015/oct/25/six-reasons-why-syrians-are-fleeing-to-europe-in-increasing-numbers.

Foged, Mette and Giovanni Peri (2015a) How immigrants and job mobility help low-skilled workers. VOX CEPR's Policy Portal. 19 April. Available from www.voxeu.org/article/how-immigrants-and-job-mobility-help-low-skilled-workers.

_____ (2015b) Immigrants' effect on native workers: new analysis on longitudinal data. Discussion Paper Series No. 8961. March. Bonn: Institute for the Study of Labour (IZA). Available from http://ftp.iza.org/dp8961.pdf. Fratzscher, Marcel and Simon Junke (2015). Integrating refugees: a long-term, worthwhile investment. DIW Economic Bulletin 45+46.2015. 12 November. Berlin: Deutsches Institut fuer Wirtschaftsforschung. Available from www.diw.de/documents/publikationen/73/diw_01.c.519306.de/diw_econ_bull_2015-45-4.pdf.

Hatton, T. J. and J. Moloney (2015). "Determinants of Applications for Asylum: Modelling Asylum Claims by Origin and Destination", CEPR Discussion Paper 10678, June. Available from https://www.cbe.anu.edu.au/ research papers/econ/wp625.pdf.

Hüttl, Pia and Alvaro Leandro (2015). How will refugees affect European economies? 19 October. Bruegel blogpost. Available from http://bruegel.org/2015/10/how-will-refugees-affect-european-economies.

Information Newsline (1999). "Iraq surveys show 'humanitarian emergency' ", United Nations Children's Fund (UNICEF), 12 August. Available from www.unicef.org/newsline/99pr29.htm.

International Labour Organization (2014) Skills mismatch in Europe. Statistics brief. September. Geneva: International Labour Office. Available from www.ilo.org/wcmsp5/groups/public/---dgreports/---stat/documents/ publication/wcms_315623.pdf.

Kassam, Ashifa, and others (2015). "Europe needs many more babies to avert a population disaster", The Guardian, 23 August. Available from www.theguardian.com/world/2015/aug/23/baby-crisis-europe-brink-depopulation-disaster.

Kaya, Bülent (2002). The changing face of Europe – population flows in the 20th century. February. Strasbourg: Council of Europe. Available from http://www.coe.int/t/dg4/education/historyteaching/Source/Projects/DocumentsTwentyCentury/Population_en.pdf.

Mohamed, A., (2015). "The ISIS Economy: Lasting and expanding", December. Beirut: Lebanese American University.

Syrian Arab Republic, Ministry of Social Affairs and Labour (2012). Official Statistics.

Office of the United Nations High Commissioner for Refugees (UNCHR) (2000). "Flight from Indochina" in The State of the World's Refugees. 1 January. Geneva: UNHCR. Available from www.unhcr.org/3ebf9bad0.pdf.

_____ (2016a) Syria Regional Refugee Response. Available from http://data.unhcr.org/syrianrefugees/ regional.php. Accessed 1 February 2016.

_____(2016b) High Commissioner welcomes Turkish work permits for Syrian refugees. 18 January. Available from www.unhcr.org/569ca19c6.html.

_____ (2016c) UNHCR Observations on the proposed amendments to the Danish Aliens legislation, L 87. Available from www.unhcr-northerneurope.org/fileadmin/user_upload/Documents/PDF/Denmark/UNHCR_ Comments_on_Danish_law_proposal_L87_January_2016.pdf.

_____(n.d.) Resettlement: A new beginning in a third country. Available from: http://www.unhcr.org/pages/4a16b1676.html

Organization for Economic Cooperation and Development (2013) International Migration Outlook 2013. 13 June. Paris: OECD Publishing.

Ott, Eleanor (2013). The labour market integration of resettled refugees. November. Geneva: UNCHR. Available from www.unhcr.org/5273a9e89.pdf.

Pinzler, Petra and Mark Schieritz (2015). "Wir werden leichter an eine Putzkraft kommen", Die Zeit, 8 October. Available from www.zeit.de/2015/41/hans-werner-sinn-fluechtlinge-deutschland-folgen.

Popal, G. R. (2000). "Impact of sanctions on the population of Iraq", Eastern Mediterranean Health Journal, July. Available from http://www.academia.edu/6403015/Eastern_Mediterranean_Health_Journal.

Portela, Clara (2012). The EU sanctions against Syria: conflict management by other means? UNISCI Discussion Papers (30),151-158. October. Available from http://ink.library.smu.edu.sg/cgi/viewcontent.cgi?article=2433&-context=soss_research.

Reliefweb (2015). No lost generation: 2015 Syria crisis update. Available from http://reliefweb.int/sites/relief-web.int/files/resources/No%20Lost%20Generation%202015%20Syria%20Crisis%20Report_FINAL.pdf.

Ruist, Joakim (2016). Fiscal cost of refugees in Europe. VOX – Centre for Economic Policy Research (CEPR) Policy Portal. 28 January. Available from www.voxeu.org/article/fiscal-cost-refugees-europe.

Syrian Center for Policy Research (2016). Confronting Fragmentation! Impact of Syrian Crisis Report. Available from http://scpr-syria.org/publications/policy-reports/confronting-fragmentation.

Thompson, Edwina (2015). Technical assessment: humanitarian use of hawala in Syria. 31 July. London: Beech-wood International. Available from http://documents.wfp.org/stellent/groups/public/documents/op_reports/wfp280155.pdf.

Tomkiw, Lydia (2015). "Refugee crisis 2015: could Syrians help Europe's aging population problem?", International Business Times, 9 October. Available from www.ibtimes.com/refugee-crisis-2015-could-syrians-help-europes-aging-population-problem-2091181.

UN Comtrade Database. Available from http://comtrade.un.org.

UNHCR and United Nations Development Programme (UNDP) (n.d.). 3RP: A strategic shift. Available from www.3rpsyriacrisis.org/the-3rp.

United Nations Children's Fund (UNICEF) (2015) Education under Fire. How conflict in the Middle East is depriving children of their schooling. 3 September. Amman: UNICEF Regional Office for the Middle East and North Africa. Available from www.unicef.org/education/files/EDUCATION-under-fire-September-2015.pdf.

UNDP (2006). Macroeconomic Policies for Poverty Reduction in Syria.

_____ (2008). Post-Conflict Economic Recovery: Enabling Local Ingenuity.

_____ (n.d.a) 3RP: Regional Refugee and Resilience Plan (2015-2016) Available from www.arabstates.undp.org/content/rbas/en/home/ourwork/SyriaCrisis/projects/3rp.html.

_____ (n.d.b). 3RP Regional Refugee & Resilience Plan 2016-2017: In response to the Syria crisis.

United Nations, Economic and Social Commission for Western Asia (ESCWA) and International Organization for Migration (IOM) (2015). 2015 Situation Report on International Migration: Migration, Displacement and Development in a Changing Arab Region. E/ESCWA/SDD/2015/1.

United Nations, ESCWA (2014a). Arab Middle Class: Measurement and Role in Driving Change. E/ESCWA/EDGD/2014/2.

_____ (2014b) Conflict in the Syrian Arab Republic: Macroeconomic Implications and Obstacles to Achieving the Millennium Development Goals. E/ESCWA/EDGD/2014/Technical Paper.5.

_____ (2015). The Impact of Sanctions on Agriculture Sector in Syria. The National Agenda for the Future of Syria programme.

United Nations, ESCWA, and League of Arab States (2013). The Arab Millennium Development Goals Report: Facing Challenges and Looking beyond 2015. E/ESCWA/EDGD/2013/1.

United Nations, Human Rights Council (2012). Thematic study of the Office of the United Nations High Commissioner for Human Rights on the impact of unilateral coercive measures on the enjoyment of human rights, including recommendations on actions aimed at ending such measures. A/HRC/19/33.

United Nations News Centre (2016). "Record $10 billion pledged in humanitarian aid for Syria at UN co-hosted conference in London", 4 February. Available from www.un.org/apps/news/story.asp?NewsID=53162#.VsBJz-PI97ak.

United Nations, Office for the Coordination of Humanitarian Affairs (OCHA) (n.d.). Syrian Arab Republic. Available from www.unocha.org/syria.

_____ (2015). Humanitarian response plan: January-December 2016. Syrian Arab Republic. Available from http://reliefweb.int/sites/reliefweb.int/files/resources/2016_hrp_syrian_arab_republic.pdf.

United Nations, Office of the High Commissioner for Human Rights (n.d.). Proceedings of the workshop on the application of unilateral coercive measures on the enjoyment of human rights by the affected populations, in particular their socioeconomic impact on women and children, in the States targeted. A/HRC/27/32.

United Nations Security Council (2015). Report of the Secretary-General on the implementation of Security Council resolutions 2139 (2014), 2165 (2014) and 2191 (2014). S/2015/962.

United Nations Secretary-General (2016). Secretary-General's opening remarks at joint press conference: supporting Syria and the region. Available from www.un.org/sg/offthecuff/index.asp?nid=4360.

United States, Department of the Treasury. Registration of non-governmental organizations ("NGOs"). Available from https://www.treasury.gov/resource-center/sanctions/Documents/ngo_guide.pdf.

Van Bergeijk, Peter A. G. (2012). Failure and success of economic sanctions. VOX – Centre for Economic Policy Research (CEPR) Policy Portal. 27 March. Available from www.voxeu.org/article/do-economic-sanctions-make-sense.

Walker, Justine, and others (2016). Unintended consequences of sanctions for humanitarian aid delivery. Report prepared for United Nations round table meeting in Beirut, 29 March.

Weaver, Matthew, Mark Tran and Emily Townsend (2016) "Syrian donor conference: more than $10bn raised, says Cameron – as it happened", The Guardian, 4 February. Available from www.theguardian.com/world/live/2016/feb/04/syrians-donor-london-conference-aid.

Wintour, Patrick and Ian Black (2016). "David Miliband calls for 1m work permits for Syrian refugees", The Guardian, 2 February. Available from www.theguardian.com/world/2016/feb/01/david-miliband-million-work-permits-syrian-refugees.

Witte, Griff and Anthony Faiola (2016) "Spring could bring a fresh surge of refugees. But Europe isn't ready for them", The Washington Post, 16 February. Available from https://www.washingtonpost.com/world/europe/spring-could-bring-a-fresh-surge-of-refugees-but-europe-isnt-ready-for-them/2016/02/16/7258c1ac-d046-11e5-90d3-34c2c42653ac_story.html.

World Food Programme (2015a). Food Security Assessment Report, Syria. October.

_____ (2015b). Market Price Watch Bulletin. Issue 2. November.

Zeit Online (2015). Wie viele Flüchtlinge können wir uns leisten? Available from http://blog.zeit.de/herdentrieb/2015/09/10/wie-viele-fluechtlinge-koennen-wir-uns-leisten_8840.

ENDNOTES

[1] Syrian Center for Policy Research (SCPR), 2016.

[2] Ibid.

[3] Cook et al, 2016.

[4] Syrian Ministry of Social Affairs and Labour, 2012.

[5] Barut, 2013.

[6] Deeb, 2011.

[7] United Nations and League of Arab States, 2013.

[8] Abu-Ismail and El-Laithy, 2010.

[9] UNDP, 2006

[10] ESCWA calculations based on Central Bank of Syria statistical abstract.

[11] ESCWA calculations based on Syrian Ministry of Finance data.

[12] ESCWA calculations based on Central Bank of Syria data.

[13] ESCWA, 2014a

[14] GDP loss was estimated by measuring the difference between estimated real GDP levels in 2010 prices during the crisis and planned GDP according to the eleventh Five Year Plan (2011-2015), had the crisis not occurred.

[15] Capital loss estimates do not include damage to military, security and police units.

[16] ESCWA, 2014b.

[17] ESCWA, 2015.

[18] World Food Programme (WFP), 2015a. To measure food security, WFP uses a composite index of three sub-indicators: a food consumption index, which measures the frequency of food consumption and diversity by families for one or more of the following goods (grains, meat, milk and dairy products, vegetables, fruits, oils, ghee and sugar); a food poverty line, which is the cost of the daily consumption of calories or cost of the food basket necessary to provide certain dietary energy requirements per individual; and an index on the use by households of resources (such as income, borrowings, savings, the sale of assets and begging) to meet dietary energy needs.

[19] Subsidies on basic goods such as oil products, bread, drinking water and cooking gas are expected to continue to fall in 2016.

[20] Oil production in Syria fell from 160,000 barrels a day in 2012 to less than 10,000 in 2015.

[21] Tariffs were reduced on average by 37 per cent in 2014. The steepest tariffs on luxury cars, jewelry and durable goods decreased from 135 per cent to 30 per cent. In 2015, tariffs on many manufacturing raw materials were unified at 5 per cent.

[22] The rate of trade deficit relative to nominal GDP is usual a key economic indicator. It is, however, less reliable in times of war, with the fall in value of the local currency and war-induced price inflation.

[23] UN Comtrade Database.

[24] ESCWA calculations based on the 2014 Central Bureau of Statistics population survey.

[25] The upper poverty line is equal to per capita expenditure on basic food needs (food poverty line) plus per capita non-food expenditure of households whose per capita food expenditure is close to the food poverty line.

[26] ESCWA calculations, assuming fixed consumption pattern for households based on 2009 data.

[27] Poverty gap is the mean shortfall of the total population from the poverty line (counting the non-poor as having zero shortfall), expressed as a percentage of the poverty line. It reflects the depth and incidence of poverty.

[28]ESCWA calculations based on the 2014 Central Bureau of Statistics population survey.

[29]ESCWA calculations based on Syrian general budget data.

[30]United Nations Children's Fund (UNICEF), 2015.

[31]ESCWA calculations based on data from the Syrian Ministry of Education and the 2014 Central Bureau of Statistics population survey.

[32]ESCWA calculations based on the 2014 Central Bureau of Statistics population survey.

[33]ESCWA calculations based on Syrian general budget data.

[34]ESCWA calculations based on data from the Syrian Ministry of Health and the 2014 Central Bureau of Statistics population survey.

[35]Delegation of the European Union to Syria.

[36] European Commission, n.d.b.

[37] Council of the European Union, 2011; European Commission, n.d.b and 2015i.

[38] European Commission, n.d.b.

[39] United Nations Secretary-General, 2016; Weaver et al, 2016.

[40]United Nations News Centre, 2016.

[41] ESCWA and IOM, 2015

[42] European Commission, 2016b.

[43]European Commission, 2016b and 2016d.

[44] European Commission, 2016c.

[45]United Nations Development Programme (UNDP), n.d.

[46]See www.3rpsyriacrisis.org.

[47] See http://ec.europa.eu/echo/files/aid/countries/factsheets/thematic/eu_children_of_peace_en.pdf.

[48]See http://nolostgeneration.org.

[49] United Nations News Centre, 2016.

[50] Fleming, 2015.

[51]UNHCR, 2016b.

[52]Wintour and Black, 2016.

[53]See http://ddc.com.jo/mafraq1/User_Site/template/View_Article.aspx?type=2&ID=272

[54]Collier, 2015.

[55]UNHCR, n.d.

[56]United Nations Office for the Coordination of Humanitarian Affairs (OCHA), n.d., UNHCR, 2016a.

[57]Chokshi, 2016.

[58] European Commission, 2015i and MPC, n.d..

[59]De La Baume, 2016; European Commission, 2016e.

[60] Barker, 2015; European Commission, 2015g and 2015h.

[61] European Commission, 2016e.

[62]UNHCR, 2016c.

[63]Zeit Online, 2015.

[64] Fratzscher and Junke, 2015.

[65]Hüttl and Leandro, 2015; Aiyar et al, 2016.

[66]Pinzler und Schieritz, 2015; Foged and Peri, 2015b.

[67] Foged and Peri, 2015a.

[68]Ruist, 2016.

[69]European Commission, 2015e.

[70] European Commission, 2014.

[71]Aiyar et al, 2016.

[72]Tomkiw, 2015.

[73]ILO, 2014.

[74]Kassam et al, 2015.

[75]Dettmer et al, 2015.

[76]Ott, 2013.

[77]Aiyar et al, 2016.

[78] Betts et al, 2014.

[79]Hatton and Moloney, 2015.

[80]European Commission, 2016a and 2015d.

[81] European Commission, n.d.a.

[82]Directorate General for Internal Policies, 2013.

[83]Council of the European Union, 2015.

[84] For more on EU sanctions see, European Commission, 2015f.

[85] For more information on United States sanctions, see www.state.gov/e/eb/tfs/spi/syria and https://www.treasury.gov/resource-center/sanctions/Programs/pages/syria.aspx. See also Walker et al,2016.

[86]Van Bergeijk, 2012.

[87]ESCWA, 2014b.

[88]Information Newsline (UNICEF), 1999.

[89]Popal, 2000.

[90]Interviews conducted by the author in December 2015–February 2016 with European doctors in Government and non-Government held areas of Syria.

[91] Walker et al, 2016.

[92]European Union External Action, n.d.

[93]Interviews, December 2015–February 2016.

[94]Interview conducted by the author in Brussels with a representative of an EU-based multinational power sector company, February 2016.

[95] British Bankers Association, 2014a.

[96] Thompson, 2015.

[97]Interviews conducted by the author in December 2015-February 2016 with representatives of international and local NGOs operating in Syria.

[98] The Financial Action Task Force (FATF) is the intergovernmental body tasked with developing and promoting policies to combat money-laundering and terrorist financing. See www.fatf-gafi.org.

[99]Thompson, 2015.

[100] Checchi and Robinson, 2013.

[101] See www.treasury.gov/resource-center/sanctions/Documents/ngo_guide.pdf.

[102] See for example British Bankers Association, 2014b.

UNDP, 2008.